Academic Vocabulary Practice
Grade 5

Credits
Content Editor: Christine Schwab
Copy Editor: Julie B. Killian

 Visit *carsondellosa.com* for correlations to Common Core, state, national, and
Canadian provincial st

Carson-Dellosa Publishing, LLC
PO Box 35665
Greensboro, NC 27425 USA
carsondellosa.com

ISBN 978-1-4838-1122-2
01-135141151

Table of Contents

Introduction

The Academic Vocabulary Practice Series

Research shows that a firm knowledge of academic vocabulary is one of the strongest indicators of a student's success in the content areas. Academic Vocabulary Practice is a series that provides students with the resources they need to build crucial vocabulary skills for success in school. The series promotes and supports literacy in: math, science, technology, language arts, social studies, geography, civics and economics, and art. The reproducible pages are designed to give students extra practice using academic vocabulary. The word lists focus on subject-specific words that often challenge students because they may rarely encounter these words in everyday use.

The books align with Common Core State Standards by offering systematic practice and usage of many of the academic and domain-specific words and phrases. Teaching vocabulary to meet the Common Core State Standards is an essential component of any standards-based curriculum.

Reproducible Pages in This Book

This book presents 200+ subject-specific words that are organized by content area. Ample opportunity is given to help students learn and connect with the vocabulary in a variety of ways.

- The Vocabulary Four Square on page 4 is an essential organizer that helps students learn new words by stating word meanings in their own words, drawing pictures to represent the words, engaging with peers in word discussions, and creating context for words.
- The Explore a Word activities let students focus on one word at a time to create associations.
- The Compare Words activities show students how two or more related words are alike and different in meaning.
- The Make Connections pages help students understand the relationships between words that are commonly presented together.
- The Play with Words activities provide review in a more playful but effective learning format.

Special Features

The Game Ideas and Suggestions section includes ideas for using the flash cards (offered online) and game templates for small group or whole group activities. The Student Dictionary pages are organized by content area and support the activity pages in each section.

Online Support

To further enhance student learning, a full set of the 200+ vocabulary words are available in flash card format online at *activities.carsondellosa.com*. These will provide opportunities for additional practice and other peer activities.

Vocabulary Four Square

Use the Vocabulary Four Square to practice new words in this book.

What I Think the Word Means	Picture
Word _____	
What My Friend Thinks the Word Means	Synonyms
	Antonyms

Sentence

Important Math
Words You Need to Know

Use this list to keep track of how well you know the new words.

0 = Don't Know   1 = Know Somewhat   2 = Know Well

___ acute angle   ___ scalene triangle

___ algebra   ___ square

___ average   ___ vertex

___ circumference

___ composite

___ coordinates

___ data

___ degree

___ divisible

___ equation

___ expression

___ formula

___ frequency

___ integer

___ isosceles triangle

___ mean

___ median

___ mode

___ negative integer

___ obtuse angle

___ prime

___ ratio

___ sample

Explore a Word

Read the paragraph. Think about the meaning of the **bold** word.

It is easy to find the **circumference** of a circle or any closed arc. Just use this formula:

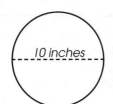

$$C = \pi \times d$$

This circle has a diameter of 10 inches.
d = 10 inches
π = 3.14
3.14 × 10 inches = 31.4 inches

1. What do you think the word means? Write your idea.

   circumference: _____

   _____

2. Write a sentence with the word **circumference**. Show what it means.

   _____

   _____

3. Check the meaning of **circumference** in the Student Dictionary.

4. If your sentence in number 2 above matches the meaning, place a ✓ after it. If your sentence does not match the meaning, write a better sentence.

   _____

   _____

5. Find the **circumference** of each circle.

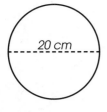 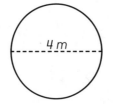 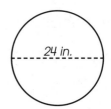

_____   _____   _____

Academic Vocabulary Practice • Grade 5 • CD-104810

Compare Words

Read the paragraphs. Think about the meaning of each **bold** word. Then, check the Student Dictionary.

Can you tell the difference between an **equation** and an **expression**? They may seem similar but are two different things.

An expression is a *mathematical phrase* that stands for a particular number.

$3 + 5$ $23 - 6$ $\frac{3}{4} \times \frac{1}{2}$

An equation is a *mathematical sentence* that shows that two things are equal. It can be true or false.

$\frac{1}{3} + \frac{1}{3} = \frac{2}{3}$ $y - 10 = 10 + x$ $(7 \times 3) - (6 \times 2) = 21 - 12$

Write *equation* or *expression* in front of each statement.

_____ 1. $33 \div 11$

_____ 2. $19 + y$

_____ 3. $\frac{(32 - 12)}{5} = 4$

_____ 4. $(3 \times 4) + (5 \times 6)$

_____ 5. $\frac{3}{4} + \frac{1}{4} = 1$

_____ 6. $\frac{10}{2} \times \frac{8}{4} = 10$

_____ 7. $0.3 + 1.7$

_____ 8. $36 + 4 = 2 \times 20$

_____ 9. $16 \div 8$

_____ 10. $\frac{24}{8}$

_____ 11. $5x - 5y = 5z$

_____ 12. $17x$

 Challenge!

The root *equ-* means "equal or same." The word *equation* means that two parts of a mathematical sentence are equal. Write other words that begin with the same root. Add a definition for each.

_____

_____

_____

Compare Words

Read the paragraph. Think about the meaning of each **bold** word. Then, check the Student Dictionary.

> Imagine that you are riding a bus to a city that is 180 miles away. The bus travels at a rate of about 60 miles per hour. How long will your trip last? Use the **formula** $d = r \times t$ (distance = rate × time). Then, use **algebra** to figure out the unknown number for t: $180 = 60 \times t$. (Answer: $t = 3$ hours)

Fill in the chart to show your understanding of each word.

	formula	algebra
What Is It?		
What I Picture		
Why Is It Important?		

Make Connections

Read the paragraph. Think about the meaning of each **bold** word. Then, check the Student Dictionary.

> A **prime** number is **divisible** by two numbers, 1 and itself. Those numbers are its factors. A **composite** number has more than two factors. A **square** number is the number you get when a number is multiplied by itself.

Fill in the blanks.

1. List all of the factors for 6. _____
   Is 6 a prime or composite number? _____

2. List all of the factors for 9. _____
   Is 9 a prime or composite number? _____

3. List all of the factors for 21. _____
   Is 21 a prime or composite number? _____

4. List all of the factors for 36. _____
   Is 36 a prime or composite number? _____

5. List all of the factors for 37. _____
   Is 37 a prime or composite number? _____

6. List all of the factors for 81. _____
   Is 81 a prime or composite number? _____

7. List all of the factors for 25. _____
   Is 25 a prime or composite number? _____

8. List all of the factors for 47. _____
   Is 47 a prime or composite number? _____

9. List all of the numbers above that are square numbers. _____

 Challenge!

Get together with a partner. List all of the prime numbers up to 200.

_____

_____

Make Connections

Look at the diagram and caption. Think about the meaning of each **bold** term. Then, check the Student Dictionary.

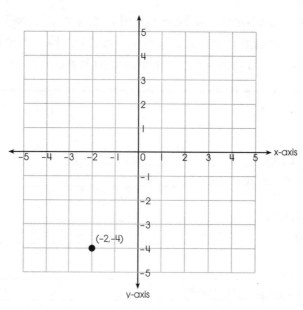

Two number lines meet at the **coordinates** (0,0). The numbers called **integers** are shown on both number lines. **Negative integers** are less than zero. The coordinates (−2,− 4) name a point where two negative integers meet.

Circle *Yes* or *No* for each question. Write your reason on the line.

1. Is zero an integer?   Yes   No

_____

2. Could the coordinates (1,−5) be shown on this grid?   Yes   No

_____

3. Could negative integers be fractions?   Yes   No

_____

4. Are the coordinates (1,−1) and (−1,1) the same?   Yes   No

_____

5. Is 150 an integer?   Yes   No

_____

Make Connections

Read the paragraph. Think about the meaning of each **bold** word. Then, check the Student Dictionary.

> Suppose you are gathering **data** about students' favorite places to visit. You can't ask every student, so you'll have to choose a **sample** of people. You'll also need to show the **frequency** of each choice. You might decide to express your findings as a **ratio** such as "Two of three students prefer to visit the science museum over the art museum."

Underline the correct ending to each sentence.

1. Frequency has to do with
   A. the number of rainy days each month this year.
   B. the amount of rain in a measuring device.

2. Data about popular places to visit can be shown in
   A. a bar graph or a circle graph.
   B. a captioned photograph.

3. The frequencies of three events labeled X, Y, and Z are shown in this pattern:

   XXYYYYZZ

   One way to state a ratio for the list is
   A. "X and Z are 4."
   B. "X is to Y as 2 is to 4."

4. Scientists would need a sample of people
   A. to test a medicine.
   B. for a trip to a space station.

5. Scientists try to gather data from samples that
   A. are typical of the whole.
   B. show the results of an experiment.

6. A ratio is like
   A. a graph that shows change over time.
   B. a fraction that shows part of a whole.

Make Connections

Read the chart and the paragraph. Think about the meaning of each **bold** word. Then, check the Student Dictionary.

Carla's Math Test Scores

Test 1	90%
Test 2	85%
Test 3	90%
Test 4	90%
Test 5	75%
Test 6	78%
Test 7	100%

Carla's **average** test score, also called the **mean**, is found by adding the seven scores and dividing by 7. The mean test score is 87%. If the scores were listed from lowest to highest, the **median** would be the middle number. The median test score is 90%. The **mode** is the number that appears most often. The mode is 90%.

Circle *Yes* or *No* for each question. Write your reason on the line.

1. Is the median price of something the same as the average price?   Yes   No

    _____

2. Is the average figured out in the same way as the mean?   Yes   No

    _____

3. Does every list of numerical data have a mode?   Yes   No

    _____

4. Could the mean be greater than the highest number in a list?   Yes   No

    _____

5. Could the mean and the median be the same number?   Yes   No

    _____

6. If five of your test scores were 95%, but one test score was 72%,
    would you want your final grade to be based on the median score?   Yes   No

    _____

Name _____

Make Connections

Look at the pictures and read the captions. Think about the meaning of each **bold** term. Then, check the Student Dictionary.

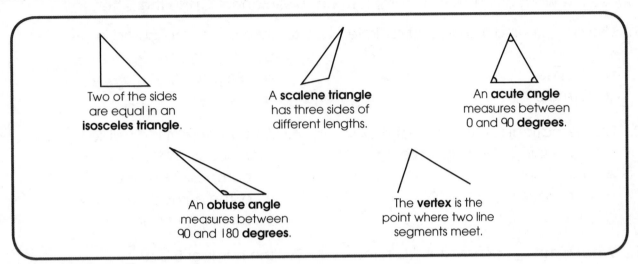

Two of the sides are equal in an **isosceles triangle**.

A **scalene triangle** has three sides of different lengths.

An **acute angle** measures between 0 and 90 **degrees**.

An **obtuse angle** measures between 90 and 180 **degrees**.

The **vertex** is the point where two line segments meet.

Follow each instruction.

1. Draw an isosceles triangle with an obtuse angle at a vertex.

2. Draw a scalene triangle with three acute angles.

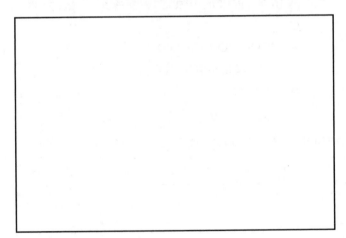

3. Draw a figure with four angles of 90 degrees each.

Play with Words

Code Words

Choose the word or words that complete each sentence. Circle the letter.

1. Use a ___ to find the area of a circle.
   - **e** frequency
   - **f** degree
   - **g** formula

2. Mathematical sentences that show that two things are equal are ___.
   - **e** equations
   - **f** averages
   - **g** primes

3. What is the ___ of boys to girls in the class?
   - **n** median
   - **o** ratio
   - **p** vertex

4. Use a ___ to locate a point on a map.
   - **l** a circumference
   - **m** coordinates
   - **n** algebra

5. Angles are measured in ___.
   - **c** integers
   - **d** algebra
   - **e** degrees

6. A number that is divisible by more than two numbers is a ___.
   - **t** composite number
   - **u** prime number
   - **v** square number

7. The number 5 is a ___.
   - **p** mode
   - **q** negative integer
   - **r** prime number

8. A triangle that has two equal sides is a ___.
   - **x** scalene triangle
   - **y** isosceles triangle
   - **z** vertex

Write the circled letters in order to find a word that names a main topic in mathematics.

_____

Play with Words

Letter by Letter

Choose the word that fits with each clue. Write it letter by letter. Some letters will be inside circles.

acute	frequency	vertex	formula	mode
isosceles	integer	obtuse	mathematics	sample

1. The number of events counted   — — — — — — — — ⃝

2. The most common number in a set of data   — ⃝ — —

3. An angle smaller than a right angle   — — ⃝ — —

4. The top of a pyramid   — — ⃝ — —

5. Example: area = length × width   — — — ⃝ — — —

6. A kind of triangle   — — ⃝ — — — — — —

7. An angle that measures 90 to 180 degrees   — — ⃝ — — —

8. The subject of this section   — — — ⃝ — — — — — — —

9. Select this to gather data.   — — — — — ⃝

10. One of these: ⁻3, ⁻2, ⁻1, 0, +1, +2, +3   — — — — — — — ⃝

Write the circled letters in order in the blanks to find the answer to this riddle.

If your uncle's sister is not your aunt, who is she?

— — — —   — — — — — — —

Important Science
Words You Need to Know

Use this list to keep track of how well you know the new words.

0 = Don't Know   1 = Know Somewhat   2 = Know Well

___ air pressure
___ anther
___ atmosphere
___ atom
___ carbon dioxide
___ chlorophyll
___ compound
___ conclusion
___ conduction
___ convection
___ electromagnetic spectrum
___ electron
___ element
___ filament
___ hypothesis
___ igneous
___ lens
___ ligament
___ metamorphic
___ molecule
___ motor
___ nerve
___ neuron

___ opaque
___ ovary
___ petal
___ photosynthesis
___ prism
___ radiation
___ reflection
___ refraction
___ sedimentary
___ sensory
___ sepal
___ spinal cord
___ stamen
___ stigma
___ style
___ tendon
___ tissue
___ translucent
___ transparent
___ vertebrae
___ visible light
___ wavelength

Explore a Word

Read the paragraph. Think about the meaning of each **bold** word. Then, check the Student Dictionary.

> The weight of air in Earth's **atmosphere** pushes downward. Even though you do not feel the air's weight on top of your head, you can feel it changing as you climb a high hill or rise in an airplane. **Air pressure**, also called *atmospheric pressure*, decreases as the distance from the Earth's surface increases.

Fill in the chart to show your understanding of each word.

	air pressure	atmosphere
What Is It?		
What I Picture		
Why Is It Important?		

Compare Words

Read the paragraph. Think about the meaning of each **bold** word. Then, check the Student Dictionary.

> Scientists use existing knowledge to try to discover new knowledge. Often, they form a **hypothesis** about what seems to be true. Then, they go through the steps of an experimental procedure. They observe and record their results. They use the results to draw a valid **conclusion**.

Complete each sentence with your own idea about a hypothesis or a conclusion.

1. The scientist's hypothesis was that the plants were dying from lack of sunlight. He reached a different conclusion after _____

    _____.

2. The mice gained a lot of weight in spite of their low-fat diet. The surprised scientist could not draw a conclusion, so she formed a new hypothesis to _____

    _____.

3. The students wanted to test the hypothesis that cutting down on high-sugar snacks would make them feel better. To draw a valid conclusion, they would have to

    _____

    _____.

4. A valid conclusion is based on analyzing test results. A good hypothesis is based on

    _____

    _____.

 Word Alert!

To name more than one hypothesis, use the plural *hypotheses*. Complete the sentences with the singular and plural forms of *hypothesis*.

Scientists have several (1.) _____ to explain the disappearance of frogs

worldwide. They have found evidence to support each (2.) _____.

Compare Words

Read the paragraph and look at the diagram. Think about the meaning of each **bold** word. Then, check the Student Dictionary.

> Muscles pull on a cord-like **tendon**, which is attached to a bone, and the bone moves as a result. Where bones meet, they are held in place with strong bands of **tissue** called **ligaments**.
>
>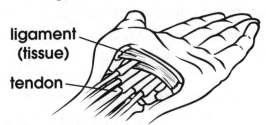
>
> ligament (tissue)
>
> tendon

Circle the word that completes each sentence.

1. One end of a (ligament, tendon) is at the end of a muscle, and the other end is attached to bone (tissue, muscle).

2. A (ligament, tendon) is like a wrapped bandage keeping bones in place.

3. A sprained ankle is the result of a tear in the (ligaments, tendons) that hold the bones of the lower leg and foot in place.

4. Many strong fibers combine to form each (ligament, tendon) that pulls on bone.

5. To move our fingers, we need the muscle-bone connections known as (ligaments, tendons).

6. (Ligaments, Tendons) in the knee joint hold the thigh bone and the shin bone together.

 Challenge!

The Achilles (uh KIL eez) tendon attaches the heel bone to the calf muscles. Achilles was a hero of Greek mythology. Research to discover how Achilles died. Use your findings to answer this question: Why is a tendon named after Achilles?

_____

_____

Name _____

Make Connections

Read the paragraph. Think about the meaning of each **bold** word. Then, check the Student Dictionary.

> Heat moves from warmer objects to cooler objects in different ways. There are three ways for heat to move, or transfer. A cool metal pan on a stove burner becomes hot as energy moves from the stove burner through the pan. This is called **conduction**. Metal is a good conductor of heat. When a pan of water is heated, the water particles at the bottom become warm and rise toward the top. The cooler water particles drop, become heated, and rise again. This circular motion is called **convection** and occurs only in liquids and gases. Heat can also be transferred through **radiation**. For example, we can feel heat from the sun without actually touching it.

Which kind of heat transfer will occur? Circle each answer.

1.	bonfire	conduction	convection	radiation
2.	hot air balloon	conduction	convection	radiation
3.	vegetable stir-fry	conduction	convection	radiation
4.	teapot	conduction	convection	radiation
5.	fireplace	conduction	convection	radiation
6.	scrambled eggs	conduction	convection	radiation

Name other examples for each kind of heat transfer.

7. conduction _____

8. convection _____

9. radiation _____

 # Word Alert!

The prefix *con-* comes from a Latin root meaning "with" or "together." Use the word *with* or *together* in a meaning for each word.

10. conform _____

11. connect _____

12. congruent _____

Academic Vocabulary Practice • Grade 5 • CD-104810

Make Connections

Read the sentences. Think about the meaning of each **bold** word. Then, check the Student Dictionary.

> A glass window is **transparent** because light rays pass through it unchanged.
>
> Frosted glass is **translucent** because light rays that pass through it change their directions.
>
> A thick curtain is **opaque** because no light passes through it.

Is each object transparent, translucent, or opaque? Circle each answer.

1.	a painted wall	transparent	translucent	opaque
2.	a clear plastic box	transparent	translucent	opaque
3.	a thin sheet of tissue paper	transparent	translucent	opaque
4.	a cardboard carton	transparent	translucent	opaque
5.	a magnifying lens	transparent	translucent	opaque
6.	waxed paper	transparent	translucent	opaque

Name two more objects that are transparent, translucent, and opaque.

7. transparent _____

8. translucent _____

9. opaque _____

 Word Alert!

The prefix *trans-* comes from a Latin root meaning "through or across." Use the word *through* or *across* in a meaning for each word.

10. translucent _____

11. transparent _____

12. transmit _____

13. transfer _____

Make Connections

Read the paragraph. Think about the meaning of each **bold** term. Then, check the Student Dictionary.

> The leaves and other green parts of a plant have cells that absorb energy from sunlight. The green chemical in the cells is called **chlorophyll**. Plants use the light energy to combine **carbon dioxide** with water to make sugar. Through this process, called **photosynthesis**, green plants make the food they need to grow and live.

Underline the correct ending to each sentence.

1. Plants get carbon dioxide from
   A. water.
   B. the air.

2. The source of energy for photosynthesis is
   A. energy from food.
   B. sunlight.

3. Chlorophyll is the reason that
   A. leaves look green.
   B. plants have cells.

4. Animals depend on photosynthesis because
   A. they can change light energy into food.
   B. they eat green plants or other animals that eat plants.

5. Chlorophyll is found in
   A. blades of grass.
   B. tree trunks.

 Look It Up!

The word *photosynthesis* is made up of two main parts. Use a classroom dictionary to find the word origin. What are the meanings of these two parts? Use words and drawings to show how the parts combine.

Name _____

Make Connections

Look at the diagram and the labels. Think about the meaning of each **bold** word. Then, check the Student Dictionary.

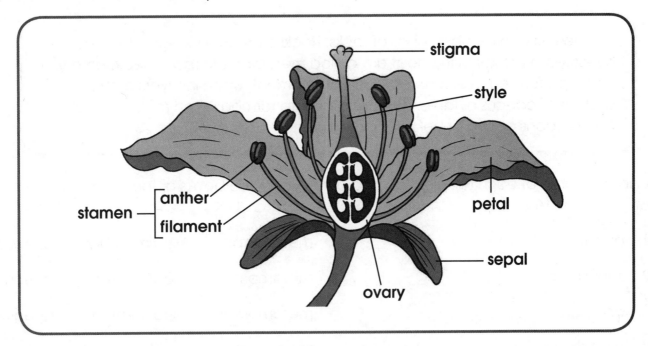

| anther | ovary | sepal | stigma |
| filament | petal | stamen | style |

Show what you know about the parts of a flower. Fill in the blanks to complete the sentences correctly. You may pluralize words if needed.

1. _____ are usually green and protect the bud.

2. Flower _____ are usually thin, soft, and brightly colored to attract insects.

3. The _____ is sticky and is at the top of the pistil.

4. The anther and the filament make up the _____ , the male part of a flower.

5. The _____ contains the egg cells.

6. The _____ is a stalk that holds the anther.

7. The _____ is above the filament and produces pollen.

8. The ovary, the stigma, and the _____ make up the pistil.

Make Connections

Read the paragraph. Think about the meaning of each **bold** word. Then, check the Student Dictionary.

> There are three basic kinds of rocks. Rocks that are changed over time by extreme pressure and heat are called **metamorphic** rocks. **Sedimentary** rocks are formed over time by layers of sediment, often in layers at the bottom of oceans or lakes. **Igneous** rocks are formed when magma cools and hardens above or below Earth's surface.

Read the name of each rock. Which kind of rock is it? Use books or the Internet to find out. Circle the answer.

1. quartzite	metamorphic	sedimentary	igneous
2. sandstone	metamorphic	sedimentary	igneous
3. obsidian	metamorphic	sedimentary	igneous
4. marble	metamorphic	sedimentary	igneous
5. tuff	metamorphic	sedimentary	igneous
6. chalk	metamorphic	sedimentary	igneous

Name other examples for each kind of rock.

7. metamorphic _____

8. sedimentary _____

9. igneous _____

Write **T** for true or **F** for false.

10. _____ Three kinds of rock make up the Earth's core.

11. _____ Most rocks that you see on the ground are sedimentary.

12. _____ All rocks are made of minerals.

Make Connections

Read the paragraphs. Think about the meaning of each **bold** word. Then, check the Student Dictionary.

> Extremely tiny particles spin around the center, or nucleus, of an **atom**. These particles have a negative charge and are called **electrons**. Each **element**, such as oxygen or gold, has a different number of electrons in its atoms.
>
> Atoms combine to form **molecules**. A molecule of water is made of one oxygen atom and two hydrogen atoms. Water is an example of a chemical **compound**. The properties of a compound are different from the properties of the elements that make it up.

Complete each sentence with information about units of matter. Include the vocabulary word in your answer.

1. molecule
   A chemical bond can form between two atoms of oxygen and one atom of carbon, which _____

   _____.

2. electrons
   Positively charged particles called protons are in the nucleus of an atom, and

   _____

   _____.

3. compound
   Table salt, or sodium chloride, forms when the elements of sodium and chlorine

   _____

   _____.

4. element
   The atoms in carbon are different from the atoms in _____

   _____.

5. atoms
   Everything around you, from the pencil in your hand to the air you breathe, is

   _____

   _____.

Make Connections

Read the paragraphs. Think about the meaning of each **bold** term. Then, check the Student Dictionary.

> Our eyes are sensitive to the **wavelengths** of energy called **visible light**. Visible light is part of the **electromagnetic spectrum**, which also includes X-rays, ultraviolet light, and microwaves.
>
> Light rays bounce off of surfaces. This action is called **reflection**. Light also changes direction, or bends, as it passes from one substance to another. We often use a **lens** to control this **refraction** of light.
>
> Visible light has different wavelengths. We can see these bands when we pass light through a **prism**. The refraction of light as it passes through a prism results in a rainbow of colors.

Circle *Yes* or *No* for each question. Write your reason on the line.

1. Can you see your face in a shiny surface because of refraction?   Yes   No

    _____

2. Do you see all wavelengths of the electromagnetic spectrum?   Yes   No

    _____

3. Can visible light pass through a prism?   Yes   No

    _____

4. Is a magnifying lens an example of a prism?   Yes   No

    _____

5.  A straw in a glass of water looks broken when viewed from the side. Does it look broken because of refraction?   Yes   No

    _____

Make Connections

Read the paragraph. Think about the meaning of each **bold** term. Then, check the Student Dictionary.

> The bones of the spine, called **vertebrae**, protect the **spinal cord**. **Nerves** from the brain and the spinal cord travel throughout the body. Nerve fibers are made of cells called **neurons**. **Sensory** neurons pick up messages from sense organs and send impulses to the spinal cord and the brain. **Motor** nerves send impulses from the brain and the spinal cord to the muscles.

Look at the pictures. Write captions that include the vocabulary words to tell about the nervous system.

1.

_____

_____

2.

_____

_____

3.

_____

_____

4.

_____

_____

 Challenge!

The human spine has 33 vertebrae. What is each group called? Research to discover the names and the numbers. Challenge friends and family members to identify each group of vertebrae.

Play with Words

Code Words

Choose the word or words that complete each sentence. Circle the letter.

1. The ___ of a plant holds its egg cells.
    a pistil
    b stamen
    c ovary

2. A nerve cell is a ___.
    n tendon
    h neuron
    p compound

3. Green light and microwaves are in ___.
    c photosynthesis
    d visible light
    e the electromagnetic spectrum

4. A scientist tests an idea called a ___.
    l conclusion
    m hypothesis
    n ligament

5. The basic unit of all matter is the ___.
    i atom
    j molecule
    k element

6. A glass of water is ___.
    b a reflection
    c transparent
    d a molecule

7. Vertebrae protect the ___.
    a spinal cord
    b electron
    c anther

8. Spacecraft leave the Earth's ___.
    j air pressure
    k prisvm
    l atmosphere

Write the circled letters in order to find a word to describe the energy that plants produce.

_____

Play with Words

If So, Then Write

Read the instructions. Then, write the correct letter in the blank. When you finish, you should have spelled a science word.

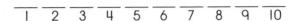

$$\overline{}\ \overline{}\ \overline{}\ \overline{}\ \overline{}\ \overline{}\ \overline{}\ \overline{}\ \overline{}\ \overline{}$$

1 2 3 4 5 6 7 8 9 10

1. If tendons are attached to muscles, write *C* on blank 1. If stamens are attached to muscles, write *L* on blank 1.

2. If refraction refers to the bending of light, write *O* on blank 2. If reflection refers to the bending of light, write *E* on blank 2.

3. If carbon dioxide is in the atmosphere, write *N* on blank 3. If chlorophyll is in the atmosphere, write *P* on blank 3.

4. If molecules are in electrons, write *S* on blank 4. If molecules are in a compound, write *C* on blank 4.

5. If vertebrae are like ligaments, write *T* on blank 5. If vertebrae surround the spinal cord, write *L* on blank 5.

6. If photosynthesis produces compounds, write *U* on blank 6. If visible light produces compounds, write *N* on blank 6.

7. If the ovary, stigma, and style make up the stamen, write *W* on blank 7. If the ovary, stigma, and style make up the pistil, write *S* on blank 7.

8. If an electron refracts light, write *M* on blank 8. If a lens refracts light, write *I* on blank 8.

9. If you can see through an opaque compound, write *A* on blank 9. If you cannot see through an opaque compound, write *O* on blank 9.

10. If a motor neuron sends a signal to move a muscle, write *N* on blank 10. If a sensory neuron sends a signal to move a ligament, write *D* on blank 10.

Important Technology Words You Need to Know

Use this list to keep track of how well you know the new words.

0 = Don't Know   1 = Know Somewhat   2 = Know Well

___ convert

___ database

___ design process

___ digital

___ friction

___ generator

___ hydroelectric

___ inertia

___ interface

___ kinetic energy

___ network

___ potential energy

___ prototype

___ receiver

___ satellite

___ spreadsheet

___ telecommunications

___ template

___ transmitter

___ troubleshooting

___ turbine

Explore a Word

Read the paragraph. Think about the meaning of the **bold** term.

> Engineers go through the steps of the **design process** to develop a new product. First, they brainstorm solutions to a problem. They choose the design idea they think will work best. They build a model and test it. Then, they redesign by going through the steps again.

1. What do you think the term means? Write your idea.

   design process: _____

   _____

2. Write a sentence with the term **design process**. Show what it means.

   _____

   _____

3. Check the meaning of **design process** in the Student Dictionary.

4. If your sentence in number 2 above matches the meaning, place a ✓ after it. If your sentence does not match the meaning, write a better sentence.

   _____

   _____

5. Make a simple drawing to show the meaning of **design process**.

Explore a Word

Read the sentences. Think about the meaning of the **bold** word. Then, check the Student Dictionary.

> The prefix *tele-* means "distance."
>
> The word *communications* names the varied ways people communicate, or send messages, to one another.
>
> **Telecommunications** are the technologies that enable communication at a distance.

Fill in the web to show your ideas about telecommunications.

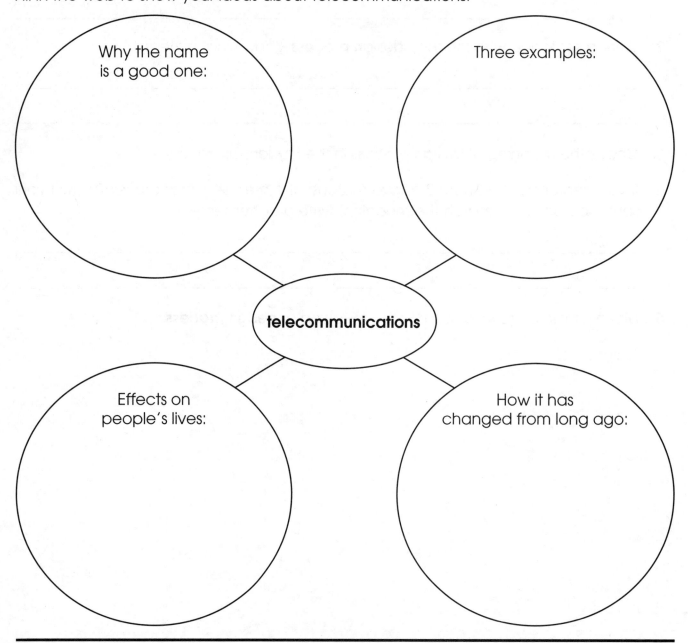

Why the name is a good one:

Three examples:

telecommunications

Effects on people's lives:

How it has changed from long ago:

Name _____

Explore a Word

Read the sentence. Think about the meaning of each **bold** word. Then, check the Student Dictionary.

> Desktop icons are part of the human-computer **interface**, designed to make a computer easy to use.

Follow each instruction.

1. Both pictures show controls for a machine. Write a caption for each picture. Use the word *interface*.

_____

_____ .

2. Use your own words to explain a "computer-printer interface."

_____ .

3. Name two features of an interface that are well designed for human operators.

_____ .

4. Complete the explanation below with a likely idea.

   The operating system on a personal computer has a GUI—a graphical user interface. The user does not type commands on a keyboard. Instead, the user gives commands by _____

   _____ .

 Word Alert!

The prefix *inter-* often means "between." What does this have to do with the meaning of *interface*?

_____

Compare Words

Read the paragraph. Think about the meaning of each **bold** word. Then, check the Student Dictionary.

> All matter has the property of **inertia**. Inertia keeps a ball resting on the ground until an outside force, such as a kick, acts on it. Inertia also keeps a ball rolling in a straight line after it is kicked. A rolling ball will eventually come to a stop. This is because its inertia has been overcome by an unseen force called **friction**.

Fill in the chart to show your understanding of the word *inertia*. Draw or write in each box.

1. Inertia is the tendency of an object at rest to stay at rest unless a force acts on it. For example:	2. When two objects have different masses, greater force is needed to overcome the inertia of the object with the greater mass. For example:
3. The force of friction acts on a moving object to overcome its inertia. For example:	4. If an object is moving, less force is needed to overcome the object's inertia slowly than to overcome it suddenly. For example:

Academic Vocabulary Practice • Grade 5 • CD-104810

Compare Words

Look at the pictures and read the captions. Think about the meaning of each **bold** term. Then, check the Student Dictionary.

potential energy   kinetic energy

Read each description. Is it an example of potential energy or kinetic energy? Circle the answer.

1. Chemical energy is stored in a log
    by a fireplace.   potential energy   kinetic energy

2. A child finishes climbing to the top of a slide.   potential energy   kinetic energy

3. An athlete uses mechanical energy to
    race around a track.   potential energy   kinetic energy

4. A battery stores chemical energy that
    can be changed to electric energy.   potential energy   kinetic energy

5. Lightning flashes in the sky.   potential energy   kinetic energy

6. Water boils in a pot on a stove.   potential energy   kinetic energy

7. Fingers hold a stretched rubber band.   potential energy   kinetic energy

8. A skateboarder gets ready to speed
    down a ramp.   potential energy   kinetic energy

 Challenge!

Kinetic energy is the energy of motion. What do you think "kinetic art" is? Write your idea. Then, check in a classroom dictionary.

_____

_____

Compare Words

Read the paragraph. Think about the meaning of each **bold** word. Then, check the Student Dictionary.

> Engineers ran tests on the **prototype** of their machine and then made improvements. Afterward, they worked with manufacturers to design **templates** for all of the parts of the machine.

Circle the word that completes each sentence.

1. You can use a standard format over and over again with a (prototype/template) in a word-processing program.

2. After making small models of the car, engineers designed a full-size (prototype/template).

3. Machines that cut patterns in metal use (prototypes/templates) to create identical patterns.

4. The main purpose of a (prototype, template) is to ensure that shapes or parts are the same.

5. Your idea for a new product sounds clever, but have you made a working (prototype/template)?

Complete the sentences with your own ideas.

6. The main reason that engineers design prototypes and templates is _____

   _____

   _____ .

7. A prototype is different from a template, however. A prototype is created so that

   _____

   _____ .

8. A template is used to _____

   _____ .

Academic Vocabulary Practice • Grade 5 • CD-104810

Compare Words

Read the paragraph. Think about the meaning of each **bold** word. Then, check the Student Dictionary.

> Use a **spreadsheet** to keep track of numbers and to perform calculations. Use a **database** to store and retrieve information.

Read each description. Is it an example from a spreadsheet or a database? Circle the answer.

1. Numbers are entered in the cells of a grid.   spreadsheet   database

2. All materials held by a library are in an
   electronic catalog.   spreadsheet   database

3. If the user changes one number, all linked
   numbers automatically adjust.   spreadsheet   database

4. A circle graph shows information about a
   household's budget.   spreadsheet   database

5. It can store millions of names, addresses,
   and phone numbers.   spreadsheet   database

6. Any American taxpayer's record of
   payments can be retrieved.   spreadsheet   database

Use your own words to explain this statement: *A spreadsheet can be used as a database.*

7. _____.

! Word Alert!

Answer each question.

8. What is spread on a sheet of paper in a spreadsheet?

   _____.

9. In what way is a database like a base, or central place, for data?

   _____.

Make Connections

Read the paragraph. Think about the meaning of each **bold** word. Then, check the Student Dictionary.

> The connected computers in the **network** all process **digital** information. When slowdown or failures occur, **troubleshooting** is needed to find and fix the problem.

Underline the correct ending to each sentence.

1. Computers are called *digital* because
   A. fingers, also called *digits*, type on keyboards.
   B. computer processing depends on the digits 1 and 0.

2. The Internet can be described as a network of
   A. email.
   B. networks.

3. The troubleshooting chapter in a computer manual shows
   A. how to run a test of the system.
   B. how to adjust the toolbar.

4. A common digital device is
   A. a clock with an hour hand and a minute hand.
   B. a clock that shows only numbers.

5. Troubleshooting is a job that
   A. engineers are trained to do.
   B. computer experts avoid.

6. A computer network in a business or a school supports
   A. the design process.
   B. telecommunication.

 Look It Up!

What is the difference between a TV network and a computer network? Look up the word *network* in a classroom dictionary. Write the meaning that fits with each definition.

7. a TV network _____

8. a computer network _____

Make Connections

Read the paragraph. Think about the meaning of each **bold** word. Then, check the Student Dictionary.

> Electronic signals are sent from the Earth to a **satellite**. The **receiver** on the satellite picks up the signals. Then, the satellite's **transmitter** sends the signals to a station on Earth.

Circle *Yes* or *No* for each question. Write your reason on the line.

1. Does a cell phone contain a transmitter?   Yes   No

   _____

2. Is a satellite held in place on a tower?   Yes   No

   _____

3. Does a home TV have a transmitter?   Yes   No

   _____

4. Could a receiver send radio signals?   Yes   No

   _____

5. Does this picture show a satellite?    Yes   No

   _____

6. Could a receiver in a car pick up satellite signals?   Yes   No

   _____

 Look It Up!

The moon is a satellite, but it is different from the kinds described on this page. Look up the word *satellite* in a classroom dictionary. What are the two main kinds of space satellites?

_____

Make Connections

Read the paragraph. Think about the meaning of each **bold** word. Then, check the Student Dictionary.

> **Hydroelectric** power comes from rushing water. As water flows from a reservoir through a dam, it makes a **turbine** spin. The spinning turbine drives a **generator** that **converts** the mechanical energy of the turbine into electrical energy.

Complete each sentence with an idea that makes sense.

1. Hydroelectric power comes from an energy source that is called *renewable* because _____

   _____ .

2. A turbine has mechanical energy because _____

   _____ .

3. A generator converts mechanical energy into _____

   _____ .

4. A turbine in a hydroelectric power plant has the job of _____

   _____ .

5. An electric generator works because of the relationship between magnetism and electricity. That is why a generator includes _____

   _____ .

6. Waterfalls can be used for hydroelectric power because _____

   _____ .

 Challenge!

Look at the three words below. What word parts do they share? Find the meanings of the word parts in a classroom dictionary. On another sheet of paper, explain what each word means using words and drawings.

hydroelectric   thermoelectric   hydrothermal

Name _____

Play with Words

Code Words

Choose the word or words that complete each sentence. Circle the letter.

1. A heavy rock is hard to move because of its ___.
   - r interface
   - s troubleshooting
   - t inertia

2. Weather forecasts depend on ___ images.
   - e satellite
   - f generator
   - g potential energy

3. A ___ sends information using signals.
   - a transmitter
   - b digital
   - c receiver

4. Anything in motion has ___.
   - i telecommunication
   - j prototypes
   - m kinetic energy

5. A ___ power station has turbines.
   - u telecommunications
   - v digital
   - w hydroelectric

6. Engineers design the ___ that allows a computer to communicate with a phone.
   - n database
   - o interface
   - p satellite

7. A ___ camera does not need film to capture light.
   - q network
   - r digital
   - s prototype

8. The ___ on a TV changes signals into audio and video.
   - j transmitter
   - k receiver
   - l network

Write the circled letters in order to find the name of an important part of the design process.

_____

Play with Words

Two at a Time

Read each clue. Find and circle the two words that match the clue.

1. a small network   w h t w o a t c o m p u t e r s i s

2. what spreadsheets do   a m a t h s l i o p e r a t i o n s g h t

3. a kind of database   a s a l i b r a r y f e a c a t a l o g t h

4. what a receiver converts   e r y e l e c t r o n i c e t s i g n a l s y o

5. steps engineers take   u c a d e s i g n n t h p r o c e s s o l d

6. what a turbine is   i t f o r o t a t i n g r t w o m a c h i n e m i

7. a program with templates   n u t w o r d e s p r o c e s s i n g y o

8. digital signals   u r b n u m e r i c a l r e a d a t a t h

Look back to find the letters you did NOT circle. Write them in order to find a riddle and its answer.

___ ___ ___   ___ ___   ___ ___   ___ ___ ___ ___   ___ ___   ___

___ ___ ___ ___ ___ ___ ___,   ___ ___ ___   ___ ___ ___   ___ ___ ___ '___

___ ___ ___ ___   ___ ___   ___ ___ ___   ___ ___ ___   ___ ___ ___ ___ ___ ___ ___ ?

(___ ___ ___ ___   ___ ___ ___ ___ ___ ___)

Academic Vocabulary Practice • Grade 5 • CD-104810

Important Language Arts Words You Need to Know

Use this list to keep track of how well you know the new words.

0 = Don't Know   1 = Know Somewhat   2 = Know Well

___ autobiography

___ bias

___ bibliography

___ colon

___ comparative

___ conclusion

___ connotation

___ drama

___ draw conclusions

___ evaluate

___ figurative language

___ flashback

___ foreshadowing

___ generalization

___ genre

___ helping verb

___ historical fiction

___ interjection

___ introduction

___ irregular verb

___ make inferences

___ myth

___ narrative

___ narrator

___ personification

___ persuasive essay

___ point of view

___ possessive pronoun

___ preposition

___ revision

___ science fiction

___ semicolon

___ superlative

___ tense

___ transition

___ verb phrase

Explore a Word

Read the sentence. Think about the meaning of each **bold** word. Then, check the Student Dictionary.

> Daniel included the **autobiography** of Hank Aaron in the **bibliography** of his report on the great ballplayer.

Fill in the chart to show your understanding of each word.

	autobiography	bibliography
What Is It?		
Questions It Answers		
Example	(a sentence or two)	(an entry)

 Word Alert!

Use the prefixes and meanings to answer the questions.

auto- ("self")	bio- ("life")	biblio- ("book")

1. Students sometimes confuse the words *bibliography* and *biography*. What is a good way to remember the difference?

   _____

2. What is the difference between a biography and an autobiography?

   _____

Compare Words

Look at the chart. Think about the meaning of each **bold** term. Then, check the Student Dictionary.

Adjective or Adverb	**Comparative** Form	**Superlative** Form
fast	faster	fastest
hot	hotter	hottest
happy	happier	happiest
happily	more happily	most happily
interesting	more interesting	most interesting
good	better	best
bad	worse	worst

Follow each instruction.

1. Use the superlative form of the adjective *white* in a sentence about laundry.

    _____

2. Use the comparative form of the adverb *loudly* in a sentence about talking.

    _____

3. Use the comparative form of the adjective *tasty* in a sentence about dessert.

    _____

4. Use the comparative and superlative forms of the adjective *good* in a sentence about sports.

    _____

5. Fix the sentence, and explain why it is incorrect.

    I just had the worsest day of my life!

    _____

    _____

    _____

Compare Words

Look at the punctuation marks and captions. Think about the meaning of each **bold** word. Then, check the Student Dictionary.

:	;
colon	**semicolon**

Complete the list of rules about using colons and semicolons. Write the correct word in each blank. Then, write the correct punctuation mark in the examples.

1. Use a _____ after the greeting in a business letter.

   Dear Ms. Ramirez   Dear Principal Marino

2. Use a _____ before a list of items or examples, or before an explanation.

   We bought several items towels, sheets, and a pillow.
   Here is my idea Let's put on a play.

3. Use a _____ to connect related statements that could be separate sentences.

   Dad is making spaghetti tonight I like spaghetti.

4. Use a _____ to separate groups of words that have commas within them.

   The tour included Paris, France, London, England, and Venice, Italy.

5. In general, use a _____ where a comma is not strong enough. Use a _____ to introduce something that follows.

 # Challenge!

Find an example of a sentence that includes both a colon and a semicolon. Copy the sentence and explain how you can tell that the marks are (or are not) used correctly.

_____

_____

Make Connections

Read the examples and the captions. Think about the meaning of each **bold** term. Then, check the Student Dictionary.

<u>Phew,</u> I'm glad that is over!	Walk <u>between</u> us, <u>over</u> the bridge, and <u>through</u> the park.	This is <u>your</u> book, but where is <u>mine</u>?
An **interjection** expresses a feeling.	A **preposition** shows a relationship and is followed by a noun or a pronoun.	A **possessive pronoun** shows ownership.

Follow each instruction.

1. Write a preposition to complete each sentence.

    I have a gift _____ my friend. The gift is _____ the table.

2. Write two interjections to express surprise.

    _____, I never saw that before! _____!

3. Write two possessive pronouns to complete the sentence.

    _____ cat is gray, and _____ is black.

4. Underline three prepositions in the sentence.

    The new book by the author is on the shelf with the others.

5. Label the interjection, the preposition, and the possessive pronoun in the sentence.

    Oh, the dog is in her bed.

Make Connections

Look at the example and read the paragraph. Think about the meaning of each **bold** term. Then, check the Student Dictionary.

> Jawan <u>has gone</u> to the store.
>
> The verb is a **verb phrase** made up of two words. The first word is the **helping verb** *has*. The main verb is the **irregular verb** *go*, which changes its form in different **tenses**.

Follow each instruction.

1. Write a sentence using the past tense of the irregular verb *swim*.

   _____

2. Underline the verb phrase in the sentence.

   Three dogs were barking.

3. Use the word *is* as a helping verb in a sentence.

   _____

4. Underline the verb phrase in the sentence. Circle the helping verb. Write the present-tense form of the irregular verb.

   Our friend had left before we arrived. _____

5. Fix the sentence and explain why it is incorrect.

   I should have went to the store myself.

   _____

 Look It Up!

Some words that look alike have different origins. These words have separately numbered entries in a dictionary. Look up the word *tense* in a classroom dictionary. In your own words, write a brief definition for each use of the word.

tense _____

tense _____

Make Connections

Read the paragraph. Think about the meaning of each **bold** word. Then, check the Student Dictionary.

> Do you know how to **evaluate** a piece of writing for **bias**? Look for opinions that are not supported by facts or logic. Look for **generalizations** that are not likely to be valid. And, look for each word that has a positive or negative **connotation**, which often reveal a bias for or against something.

Underline the correct ending to each sentence.

1. The connotation of a word is
   A. similar to its dictionary definition.   B. the feelings it suggests.

2. An example of a generalization is
   A. "Everyone needs to eat."   B. "My favorite food is broccoli."

3. A statement of bias is
   A. strong.   B. unfair.

4. When readers evaluate a written work, they might ask themselves,
   A. "Has the author done a good job?"
   B. "What are some other books on this topic?"

5. A word with a favorable connotation is
   A. *cozy*, as in "a cozy house."   B. *tiny*, as in "a tiny house."

6. A generalization that shows bias is
   A. "All students watch too much TV."
   B. "All students need ways to learn."

 # Word Alert!

Complete each sentences with a word from the word bank.

general	generally	generalize	generalization

A (1.) _____ is a statement that applies to most or all situations. Some

(2.) _____ statements are valid. It is fine to use examples and logic to

(3.) _____ about things that are (4.) _____ true.

Make Connections

Read the paragraph. Think about the meaning of each **bold** term. Then, check the Student Dictionary.

> A story is told from a particular **point of view**. The author unfolds the point of view of the **narrator** as the story develops. The story may be told from these points of view:
>
> First Person (using words such as *I, me, mine*)
>
> Second Person (using words such as *you, your*)
>
> Third Person (using words such as *he, she, it, they, them*)

Read each passage. Write the point of view from which it is written.

1. I can't wait to get home. My mother called and said that she and Dad had stopped by the Paws and Claws Pet Shoppe this morning. She wouldn't tell me any more but said their purchase would make me very happy. Oh, the clock is so slow!

    _____

2. You are on a long ride with your Uncle Matt. You think the trip is never going to end. Uncle Matt plays awful music on the radio. Plus, he sings badly. You think this is the longest road trip of your life.

    _____

3. Anton heard a strange noise coming from his closet. It sounded like a large animal chewing cardboard. He grabbed his magic wand and paused in front of the door.

    _____

4. Last month, I made a bracelet for my best friend. It fit her perfectly, and she really liked it. She wore it every day. But, today she is not wearing it. She also did not sit with me at lunch. I wonder what is going on.

    _____

5. Write your own short story. Tell what point of view you wrote it from.

    _____

    _____

    _____

Make Connections

Read the paragraphs. Think about the meaning of each **bold** term. Then, check the Student Dictionary.

> The main character's **narrative** begins with a **personification** of a house. "I live in a friendly house that has a warm lap," the narrator says. She goes on to use other **figurative language**. When she describes a meal "as tasty as a rat's tail," the reader realizes that the narrator is a cat. Her name is Kitty.
>
> The narrative includes a **flashback** to Kitty's early life, when she lived in a different, dangerous place. Kitty says, "I thought I was done with that place. But, I was wrong." This **foreshadowing** of danger adds suspense to the narrative.

Complete each sentence with information about written works. Include the vocabulary word in your answer.

1. personification
   The author writes, "Long fingers of icicles reached down from the tree branches." The comparison _____

   _____.

2. foreshadowing
   An author wants to keep a reader involved in a story, and _____

   _____.

3. figurative language
   Idioms, similes, metaphors, and _____

   _____.

4. flashback
   Sometimes, an author will hint at things to come, and sometimes _____

   _____.

5. narrative
   Sometimes, a story comes from the author's imagination, but _____

   _____.

Make Connections

Read the paragraph. Think about the meaning of each **bold** term. Then, check the Student Dictionary.

> Written works are classified as fiction, nonfiction, poetry, or **drama**. These broad **genres** include many others such as **myths**, **historical fiction**, and **science fiction**.

Circle *Yes* or *No* for each question. Write your reason on the line.

1. Is drama a play that actors perform?   Yes   No

_____

2. Is a tall tale an example of a myth?   Yes   No

_____

3. Is science fiction always set in the future?   Yes   No

_____

4. Is historical fiction always set in the past?   Yes   No

_____

5. Is a poem the same as a genre?   Yes   No

_____

6. Is a myth like a hero tale?   Yes   No

_____

7. Could Abraham Lincoln be a character in historical fiction?   Yes   No

_____

8. Could an author write a genre?   Yes   No

_____

Make Connections

Read the paragraph. Think about the meaning of each **bold** term. Then, check the Student Dictionary.

> A **persuasive essay** often follows a standard structure: an **introduction**, a body that includes clear **transitions**, and a **conclusion**. It may take several **revisions** to make those paragraphs persuasive to readers.

Use the vocabulary words to complete the paragraph. Use each word only once.

The title of Felipe's (1.) _____ was "Save Our Music." He began with a lively (2.) _____ that ended with his main idea: "We need more music in school, not less." He made sure that the relationships among his ideas were pointed out with (3.) _____ such as "first of all" and "most important." He ended with a strong (4.) _____ to sum up his arguments. Felipe said that he worked hard on the essay and went through three (5.) _____. The final version was published in the town newspaper.

 Word Alert!

The suffix -ion is added to the end of a word to form a noun. Four of the vocabulary words have the suffix -ion. What is the base word in each? Check your ideas in a classroom dictionary and then write the base words below.

_____

_____

Make Connections

Read the paragraph. Think about the meaning of each **bold** term. Then, check the Student Dictionary.

> Readers often **draw conclusions** when reading a story. They think about the details and how they add up. Then, they make decisions about what may happen next. Sometimes, readers **make inferences** about what they have read. They try to read between the lines and guess what might happen next.

Read each passage. Make an inference or draw a conclusion.

1. When I looked at the menu, I felt happy inside. All of my favorite desserts were there. The menu had a huge list of ice cream flavors. There were other specialties too, such as sundaes, banana splits, and milk shakes.

   _____

   _____

2. Sammy and Trish sat on the love seat in the corner. Trish was surprised. Sammy did not seem afraid. She sat quietly. Then, a large dog walked in with his owner. The fur on Sammy's neck stood up. She jumped off the chair and opened her mouth.

   _____

   _____

3. Juan sat in the corner seat reading a magazine. It was hard to pay attention because the screaming baby would not be comforted. And, it was gross to hear the old man's wet cough. Finally, the nurse called Juan's name.

   _____

   _____

4. The three of us were silent, concentrating hard. I tried to think of nothing but where I would be in four minutes. Then, I looked straight ahead, bent and touched my fingers on the starting line, and stretched my left leg out behind me. I waited.

   _____

   _____

Play with Words

Code Words

Choose the word or words that complete each sentence. Circle the letter.

1. The word *oops* is ___.
   l   an interjection
   m   an irregular verb
   n   a preposition

2. The book *My Life Story* is most likely ___.
   h   a bibliography
   i   an autobiography
   j   science fiction

3. Words, such as *meanwhile* and *as a result*, can show ___.
   r   a conclusion
   s   a bibliography
   t   transitions

4. Greek gods are characters in ___.
   c   genres
   d   historical fiction
   e   myths

5. The word *from* in "a card from me" is a ___.
   q   possessive pronoun
   r   preposition
   s   transition

6. A shift in a narrative to a past event is ___.
   a   a flashback
   b   foreshadowing
   c   a drama

7. The word *smelly* has a negative ___.
   p   conclusion
   q   superlative
   r   connotation

8. One kind of figurative language is ___.
   w   a possessive pronoun
   x   a verb phrase
   y   personification

Write the circled letters in order to find a word that describes a book discussion.

_____

Play with Words

For Example

Find the examples that match each vocabulary word. Write the letter of the examples in the blank.

1. prepositions ___
2. genres ___
3. helping verbs ___
4. possessive pronouns ___
5. personification ___
6. narratives ___
7. tenses ___
8. drama ___
9. superlatives ___
10. figurative language ___

g   past, present, future

w   his, your, ours

e   "the screaming wind", "a smile as cold as ice"

n   mystery, fantasy, folktale

b   biggest, strongest, happiest

d   "My Life as a Dog", an autobiography

k   as, about, from, with

l   pouting clouds, dancing leaves

o   *is* watching, *has* watched, *should have* watched

a   *Romeo and Juliet*, a TV show episode, a radio play

Write the letters in order in the blanks to find a word to find a word that just might describe you!

___ ___ ___ ___ ___ e ___ ___ e ___ ___ l ___

Important Social Studies Words You Need to Know

Use this list to keep track of how well you know the new words.

0 = Don't Know   1 = Know Somewhat   2 = Know Well

___ abolitionist

___ aggression

___ alliance

___ American Revolution

___ Articles of Confederation

___ boycott

___ Civil War

___ colonial

___ colonization

___ compromise

___ Congress

___ consequences

___ Constitution

___ Convention

___ Declaration of Independence

___ discrimination

___ Dust Bowl

___ era

___ expedition

___ Great Depression

___ Harlem Renaissance

___ Industrial Revolution

___ industrialization

___ Mayflower Compact

___ missionary

___ negotiation

___ New Deal

___ plantation

___ Reconstruction

___ republic

___ revolutionary

___ secede

___ sharecropper

___ states' rights

___ urbanization

Explore a Word

Read the sentence. Think about the meaning of the **bold** word. Then, check the Student Dictionary.

> France formed **alliances** with some of the American Indian nations, and Britain were allied with others.

Fill in the chart to show your understanding of the word *alliance*.

1. Words with meanings similar to *alliance*:	2. Examples of alliances among nations:
3. The purpose of an alliance:	4. How an alliance is made:

Explore a Word

Read the quotation. Think about the meaning of the **bold** word. Then, check the Student Dictionary.

"I pledge allegiance to the flag of the United States of America and to the **republic** for which it stands . . ."

Fill in the web to show your ideas about republics.

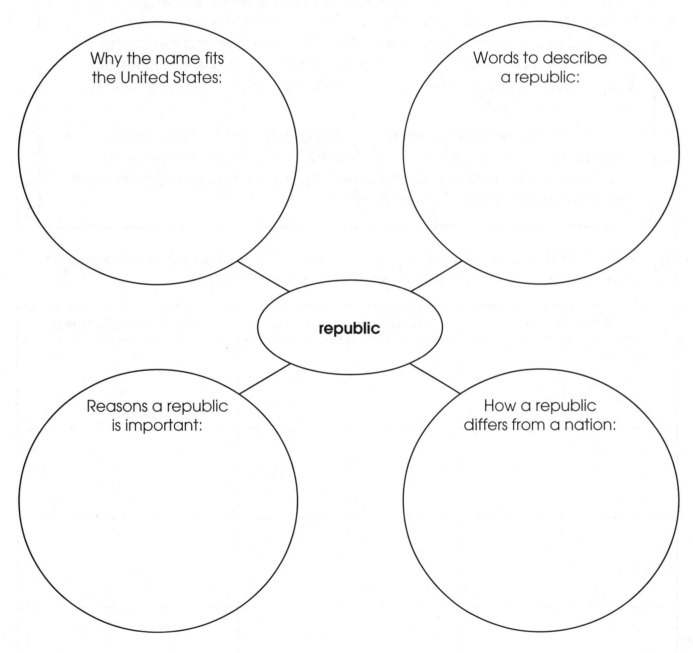

Why the name fits the United States:

Words to describe a republic:

republic

Reasons a republic is important:

How a republic differs from a nation:

Compare Words

Read the paragraphs. Think about the meaning of each **bold** word. Then, check the Student Dictionary.

> The **Mayflower Compact** was the first written plan of government in America. Forty-one English colonists signed it aboard the *Mayflower* in November 1620.
>
> More than a century later, the American colonies felt mistreated by Britain and wanted out. The **Declaration of Independence** was approved by delegates to the Second Continental **Congress** on July 4, 1776. This document marks the birth of the United States and the start of the Revolutionary War. Later, even as the war continued, the **Articles of Confederation** (approved in 1777 and ratified in 1781) finally established a central government.
>
> The Constitutional **Convention** was held in May 1787 in Philadelphia, Pennsylvania. Delegates from 12 of 13 states worked for four months on a new document called the "**Constitution**." It created a stronger government and provided more freedom for US citizens.

Fill in the KWL chart with four questions you have about the information in the passage. Research in books or online and complete the rest of the chart.

What I know	What I want to know	What I have learned

Academic Vocabulary Practice • Grade 5 • CD-104810

Compare Words

Read the paragraph. Think about the meaning of each **bold** word. Then, check the Student Dictionary.

> One nation's act of **aggression** against another is a cause of war. Through **negotiation**, however, war is sometimes prevented.

Read each description. Is it an example of aggression or negotiation? Circle the answer.

1. Pirates attacked ships carrying people and cargo.   aggression   negotiation

2. Traders exchanged manufactured goods for the animal pelts that hunters delivered.   aggression   negotiation

3. As colonists' settlements grew larger, the original inhabitants of the region were crowded out.   aggression   negotiation

4. The travelers made an agreement to follow the rule of law as they set up their new colony.   aggression   negotiation

5. Representatives of the defeated nation signed the treaty, even though the terms were harsh.   aggression   negotiation

 Word Alert!

Words that belong to the same word family have related meanings. Complete each sentence with a word from the word bank.

negotiate	negotiable	negotiation	negotiator

Both sides agreed to meet with a (1.) _____ to (2.) _____ an end to their disagreement. One by one, each (3.) _____ item was discussed. The dispute ended with a signed agreement, so the (4.) _____ was a success.

Compare Words

Read the paragraph. Think about the meaning of each **bold** word. Then, check the Student Dictionary.

> As the nation's industries grew, people from farms came to work in factories. As a result, the population of cities increased rapidly. Greater **industrialization** led to greater **urbanization**.

Complete each sentence with your own ideas about industrialization and urbanization. Explain as much as you can.

1. Industrialization leads to more jobs in factories. Urbanization occurs at the same time because _____

   _____ .

2. In the early twentieth century, signs of industrialization in the United States included factory smokestacks and railroad cars loaded with freight. Signs of urbanization included _____

   _____ .

3. One of the problems with urbanization is overcrowding, which can lead to homelessness and the easy spread of disease. One of the problems with industrialization is _____

   _____ .

4. Throughout most of history, the manufacturing of goods took place in homes and small shops. But, with industrialization and urbanization, ways of life changed. For example, _____

   _____ .

 ## Word Alert!

A suffix is a word part added to the end of a word. Each vocabulary word has more than one suffix. Write words and suffixes to complete the word equations.

5. industry + _____ + -ize + _____ = _____

6. _____ + _____ + -ation = urbanization

Make Connections

Read the paragraph. Think about the meaning of each **bold** term. Then, check the Student Dictionary.

> As a result of the **American Revolution**, colonies became independent of their foreign government. Nothing like that had ever happened before in history. The **Industrial Revolution** forever changed the ways goods were produced and the ways that people worked. Both the American Revolution and the Industrial Revolution were truly **revolutionary**.

Underline the better ending to each sentence.

1. The American Revolution was fought against
   A. colonists.
   B. Britain.

2. The Industrial Revolution had to do with
   A. the growth of factories.
   B. the end of the Middle Ages.

3. The American Revolution is also called
   A. the Revolutionary War.
   B. a revolutionary industry.

4. The founders of the United States had revolutionary
   A. independence.
   B. ideas about government.

5. Britain's colonies supplied Britain with raw materials that could be used to manufacture goods. This ready supply was one reason that the Industrial Revolution
   A. caused the American Revolution.
   B. began in Britain.

6. Businesses sometimes say that they have a revolutionary new product because they want others to think that
   A. they have fought hard to make it.
   B. the product will change the world.

Make Connections

Read the paragraph. Think about the meaning of each **bold** word. Then, check the Student Dictionary.

> Spanish rulers sponsored early **expeditions** to the Americas. Spain was the first European country with **colonial** holdings in North America. Spanish **colonization** included building forts and missions, especially in the Southwest and California. Spanish **missionaries** spread the Catholic religion to native peoples.

Circle *Yes* or *No* for each question. Write your reason on the line.

1. Is a colonial government independent?   Yes   No

    _____

2. Could Spanish colonization take place in Spain?   Yes   No

    _____

3. Could a missionary have been a monk or a priest?   Yes   No

    _____

4. Do expeditions always involve sea voyages?   Yes   No

    _____

5. Is colonization the same as settlement?   Yes   No

    _____

 Challenge!

Write one or two sentences and include all of these words: *colony, colonial, colonists, colonization.*

_____

_____

_____

Make Connections

Read the paragraph. Think about the meaning of each **bold** term. Then, check the Student Dictionary.

> **Abolitionists** wanted the South to end slavery. The South demanded that **states' rights** be protected. Attempts at **compromise** failed. Southern states **seceded** and formed their own government. The United States was torn apart during the **Civil War**.

Circle *Yes* or *No* for each question. Write your reason on the line.

1. Were supporters of states' rights against having a central government?   Yes   No

_____

2. Do people settle for less than they want if they compromise?   Yes   No

_____

3. Is seceding similar to joining?   Yes   No

_____

4. Were all abolitionists against slavery?   Yes   No

_____

5. Is the "War Between the States" the same as the Civil War?   Yes   No

_____

 Look It Up!

What is the difference between the *Civil War* and a *civil war*? Look up both terms in a classroom dictionary. Write a sentence to explain the difference.

_____

_____

Make Connections

Read the paragraphs. Think about the meaning of each **bold** word. Then, check the Student Dictionary.

> The South's defeat in the Civil War had **consequences** that lasted for more than a century. The southern states lost their right to self-government during the period known as **Reconstruction**. The **plantation** economy was destroyed. Instead, poor **sharecroppers** would struggle for generations to farm small plots of rented land.
>
> After white southerners regained control of their states, they passed laws to segregate the races. Racial **discrimination** continued for decades. The civil rights movement finally brought change. One famous and successful civil rights protest was the **boycott** of buses in Montgomery, Alabama, in 1955 and 1956.

Complete each sentence with an idea that makes sense.

1. Discrimination against a particular racial or ethnic group causes _____

   _____.

2. US laws passed during Reconstruction were intended to help former slaves _____

   _____.

3. The idea behind a boycott of a product or a service is that _____

   _____.

4. Sharecroppers were not enslaved, but their lives were _____

   _____.

5. Wars always have long-lasting consequences because _____

   _____.

6. Southern plantations were different from farms in the North. One important difference was _____

   _____.

Make Connections

Read the paragraphs. Think about the meaning of each **bold** term. Then, check the Student Dictionary.

> African American poets, writers, artists, and musicians were drawn to the New York City neighborhood of Harlem in the 1920s. This **era** of artistic expression became known as the **Harlem Renaissance**.
>
> The era was followed by one of the most difficult periods in American history, the **Great Depression**. Banks failed. Millions of workers lost their jobs. Poverty and homelessness spread. In the southern Great Plains, environmental disaster struck. Farm families lost everything in the great windstorms that blew dried-out soil throughout the **Dust Bowl**.
>
> Americans looked to their new president, Franklin D. Roosevelt, and hoped that the laws of his **New Deal** would provide "relief, recovery, and reform."

Underline the correct ending to each sentence.

1. The Harlem Renaissance was
   A. a creative time.
   B. an interesting place.

2. An example of a historic era is
   A. the immigrant cultures in New York City.
   B. the period between World War I and World War II.

3. The New Deal was the name for
   A. efforts to prevent environmental disasters.
   B. a program to pass new laws to help struggling Americans.

4. As the Great Depression began, many people
   A. decided to invest in the stock market.
   B. feared that their savings in banks would vanish.

5. The Dust Bowl was the name for
   A. dry, stormy weather.
   B. a dry region.

Play with Words

Code Words

Choose the word or words that complete each sentence. Circle the letter.

1. The expansion of cities is ___.
   g negotiation
   h urbanization
   i discrimination

2. The ___ created a stronger government and provided more freedom for US citizens.
   e Constitution
   f Declaration of Independence
   g Mayflower Compact

3. Nobody can predict all of the ___ of an event.
   q industrialization
   r consequences
   s aggression

4. Supporters of ___ want a less powerful central government.
   g abolitionists
   h the Industrial Revolution
   i states' rights

5. The US holiday of Thanksgiving began during the colonial ___.
   r missionary
   s boycott
   t era

6. A compromise may be reached after ___.
   a negotiation
   b aggression
   c an expedition

7. Citizens vote for their leaders in a ___.
   f plantation
   g republic
   h boycott

8. The ___ forever changed the way people worked.
   c American Revolution
   d New Deal
   e Industrial Revolution

Write the circled letters in order to find the answer to this question: *What does studying history help us learn?*

our _____

Play with Words

If So, Then Write

Read the instructions. Then, write the correct letter in the blank. When you finish, you should have spelled a word that names people fascinated by the past.

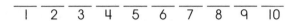

$$\overline{}\;\overline{}\;\overline{}\;\overline{}\;\overline{}\;\overline{}\;\overline{}\;\overline{}\;\overline{}\;\overline{}$$
1   2   3   4   5   6   7   8   9   10

1. If the Harlem Renaissance names a period of struggle, write *L* on blank 1. If the Harlem Renaissance names a period of creativity, write *H* on blank 1.

2. If abolitionists supported slavery, write *O* on blank 2. If abolitionists opposed slavery, write *I* on blank 2.

3. If the Great Depression happened before the Civil War, write *M* on blank 3. If Reconstruction happened after the Civil War, write *S* on blank 3.

4. If friendly nations have an alliance, write *T* on blank 4. If enemy nations have an alliance, write *C* on blank 4.

5. If aggression is like fighting, write *O* on blank 5. If aggression is the opposite of fighting, write *P* on blank 5.

6. If a boycott is supposed to have an impact on business, write *R* on blank 6. If a boycott is supposed to have an impact on immigration, write *L* on blank 6.

7. If the New Deal had to do with the transcontinental railroad, write *G* on blank 7. If the New Deal had to do with the Great Depression, write *I* on blank 7.

8. If *urbanization* means increased population of cities, write *A* on blank 8. If *urbanization* means increased population of farms, write *R* on blank 8.

9. If the American Revolution led to a republic, write *N* on blank 9. If the Industrial Revolution led to a republic, write *O* on blank 9.

10. If industrialization involved missionaries, write *E* on blank 10. If colonization involved missionaries, write *S* on blank 10.

Important Geography Words You Need to Know

Use this list to keep track of how well you know the new words.

0 = Don't Know   I = Know Somewhat   2 = Know Well

___ annexation

___ arid

___ cartographer

___ humidity

___ latitude

___ longitude

___ parallels

___ physical feature

___ political boundary

___ population density

___ prime meridian

___ projection

___ savanna

___ tectonic plates

___ terrain

___ time zone

___ tropical

Name _____

Explore a Word

Read the paragraph. Think about the meaning of the **bold** term. Then, check the Student Dictionary.

> The boundary of two of Earth's **tectonic plates** is in the middle of the Atlantic Ocean. At this boundary, the North American plate and the Eurasian plate are being pushed apart by molten rock rising from below the Earth's crust.

Follow each instruction.

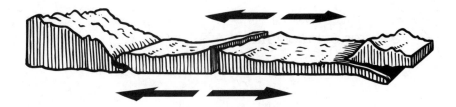

1. Write a caption to explain what is shown in the picture. Use the term *tectonic plates.*

_____

_____

2. In your own words, explain what this statement means: *The tectonic plates move continents.*

_____

3. The word *tectonic* means "having to do with movement and changes in Earth's crust." What does the word *plate* mean to Earth scientists?

_____

 Challenge!

Earth scientists use the term *tectonic plates*. They also use the term *plate tectonics*. What is the difference? Use a dictionary or other resource to find the answer. Explain the difference in your own words.

_____

_____

_____

Compare Words

Read the paragraph. Think about the meaning of each **bold** word. Then, check the Student Dictionary.

> **Terrain** describes the **physical features** of an area. For example, the terrain is hilly in one part of the state, but it is flat in other parts.

Fill in the web to show your ideas about terrains.

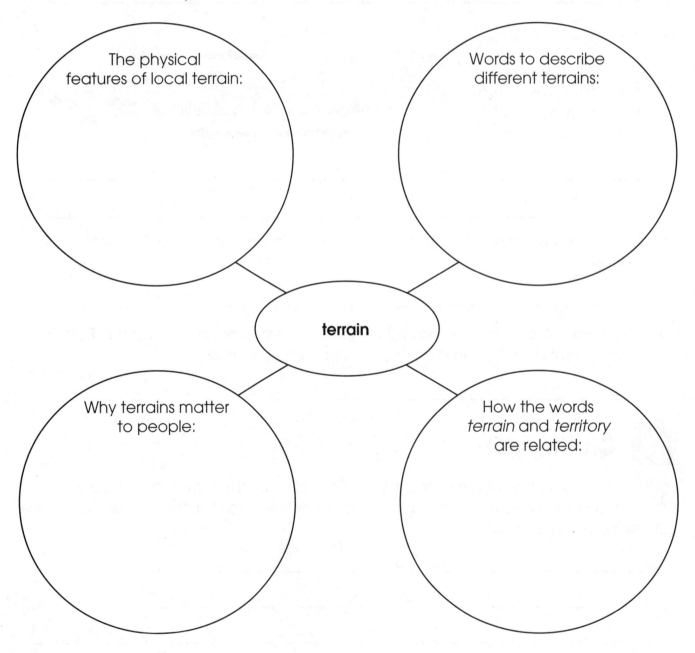

The physical features of local terrain:

Words to describe different terrains:

terrain

Why terrains matter to people:

How the words *terrain* and *territory* are related:

Compare Words

Look at the diagrams and read the captions. Think about the meaning of each **bold** word. Then, check the Student Dictionary.

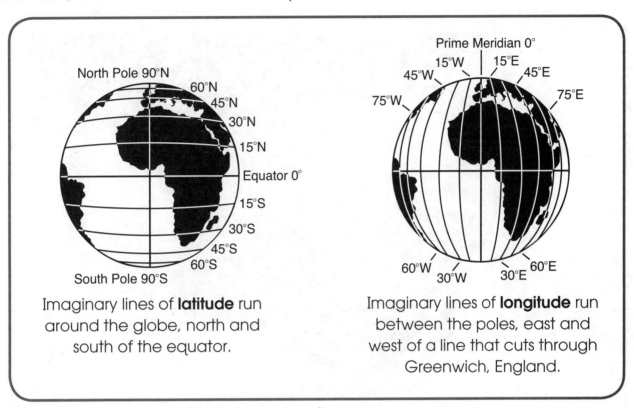

Imaginary lines of **latitude** run around the globe, north and south of the equator.

Imaginary lines of **longitude** run between the poles, east and west of a line that cuts through Greenwich, England.

Circle the word that completes each sentence.

1. The equator is at 0 degrees (latitude, longitude).

2. If you traveled in a straight line from east to west, you would change your (latitude, longitude).

3. A line of (latitude, longitude) is a half circle on the globe.

4. Locations south of Greenwich, England, could be at the same (latitude, longitude).

5. The South Pole is at 90 degrees (latitude, longitude).

6. Lines of (latitude, longitude) meet.

7. Any location in the United States has a (latitude, longitude) labeled "west."

8. The distance between any two lines of (latitude, longitude) is greatest at the equator.

Make Connections

Look at the map and read the caption. Think about the meaning of each **bold** term. Then, check the Student Dictionary.

Because Earth completes a spin every 24 hours, sunrise and sunset occur at different times throughout the world. The world is divided into 24 **time zones**. Each is 15° longitude wide, starting with the **prime meridian** at 0° in Greenwich, England. If it is noon in Greenwich, it is 7 am in New York City.

Underline the correct ending to each sentence.

1. If it is noon in New York City, it is
   A. 3 pm in Los Angeles.   B. 9 am in Los Angeles.

2. The sun sets earlier in Chicago than in
   A. Los Angeles.   B. New York City.

3. A full 360° of longitude is the same as
   A. 24 hours of time.   B. 12 hours of time.

4. Passengers flying east may need to set their watches
   A. later when they land.   B. earlier when they land.

5. Two cities at the same longitude
   A. usually have the same time.   B. never have the same time.

Name _____

Make Connections

Read the paragraphs. Think about the meaning of each **bold** word. Then, check the Student Dictionary.

> Two lines of latitude are labeled Tropic of Cancer and Tropic of Capricorn. These **parallels** are on either side of the equator. They mark Earth's **tropical** zone.
>
> Many people think that all tropical regions have high **humidity** and rain forests. But, the tropics include **arid** regions. Most of the world's **savannas** are in the tropics. These grasslands develop where there is a long dry season.

Complete each sentence with an idea that makes sense.

1. Lines of latitude are also called *parallels* because _____

   _____ .

2. Large herds of grazing animals, such as zebras and antelopes, live on African savannas. These animals are forced to _____

   _____ .

3. Tropical climates are hot year-round, but the humidity _____

   _____ .

4. Warm summers with high humidity and cold, snowy winters are found at parallels

   _____ .

5. Some regions are more arid than others. For example, _____

   _____ .

6. A savanna may be found between a rain forest and a desert. It is different from both of these regions because _____

   _____ .

Academic Vocabulary Practice • Grade 5 • CD-104810

75

Make Connections

Read the paragraphs. Think about the meaning of each **bold** term. Then, check the Student Dictionary.

> **Cartographers** face challenges as they try to "flatten" the globe to turn it into a map. Distances and shapes cannot be shown with complete accuracy on a flat map. Cartographers use **projections** to represent Earth's curved surfaces on a flat sheet of paper.
>
> Cartographers revise maps as **political boundaries** change. For example, nations may split into smaller units or grow larger through **annexation**. Cartographers create thematic maps too. Thematic maps might show climate, vegetation patterns, or **population density** in regions.

Complete each sentence with information about geography. Include the vocabulary word in your answer.

1. population density
   The country of India has a large land area. But, with more than one billion people, India _____

   _____ .

2. projection
   A map of a city can show streets and parks accurately drawn to scale. A map that shows the world's continents, however, _____

   _____ .

3. annexation
   The United States grew in size as a result of _____

   _____ .

4. political boundary
   We studied a map of Africa in which a solid line showed _____

   _____ .

Name _____

Play with Words

Code Words

Choose the word or words that complete each sentence. Circle the letter.

1. A map ___ can make a continent look stretched.
   r projection
   s tectonic plate
   t annexation

2. The boundary of two of Earth's ___ is in the middle of the Atlantic Ocean.
   a tectonic plates
   b savannas
   l terrains

3. ___ lines are imaginary.
   h Population density
   i Latitude
   j Tectonic plate

4. ___ is high in crowded cities.
   l Humidity
   m A political boundary
   n Population density

5. Global times are measured from ___.
   e a time zone
   f the prime meridian
   g a cartographer

6. Imaginary lines of ___ run around the globe north and south of the equator.
   a latitude
   b longitude
   c time zone

7. All regions lying near the equator are ___.
   h arid
   i longitude
   l tropical

8. A ___ could be covered with thick forests.
   k savanna
   l terrain
   m time zone

Write the circled letters in order to find the name of something that affects the lives of plants and animals in any region.

_____

Play with Words

If So, Then Write

Read the instructions. Then, write the correct letter in the blank. When you finish, you should have spelled the name of someone who studies the world.

$$\overline{}\ \overline{}\ \overline{}\ \overline{}\ \overline{}\ \overline{}\ \overline{}\ \overline{}\ \overline{}\ \overline{}$$
1   2   3   4   5   6   7   8   9   10

1. If terrain describes the elevation of a place, write *F* on blank 1. If terrain describes the physical features of a place, write *G* on blank 1.

2. If lines of latitude run around the globe east and west of the equator, write *T* on blank 2. If lines of latitude run around the globe north and south of the equator, write *E* on blank 2.

3. If the prime meridian is a line of longitude, write *O* on blank 3. If the prime meridian is parallel to the equator, write *I* on blank 3.

4. If a savanna is arid all year, write *P* on blank 4. If a savanna is arid for part of the year, write *G* on blank 4.

5. If the world is divided into 12 time zones, write *E* on blank 5. If the world is divided into 24 time zones, write *R* on blank 5.

6. If the equator cuts a globe in half, write *A* on blank 6. If the equator does not cut a globe in half, write *M* on blank 6.

7. If tectonic plates have to do with earthquakes, write *P* on blank 7. If tectonic plates have to do with hurricanes, write *U* on blank 7.

8. If a projection is used on a map, write *H* on blank 8. If a projection is used on a globe, write *B* on blank 8.

9. If volcanoes cause tectonic plates, write *A* on blank 9. If continents rest on tectonic plates, write *E* on blank 9.

10. If annexation affects political boundaries, write *R* on blank 10. If annexation has no effect on political boundaries, write *S* on blank 10.

Academic Vocabulary Practice • Grade 5 • CD-104810

Important Civics and Economics Words You Need to Know

Use this list to keep track of how well you know the new words.

0 = Don't Know   1 = Know Somewhat   2 = Know Well

___ amendment

___ assembly

___ assembly line

___ checks and balances

___ Congress

___ consumption

___ demand

___ distribution

___ due process

___ entrepreneur

___ executive

___ House of Representatives

___ judicial

___ majority rule

___ mass production

___ official

___ petition

___ Senate

___ specialization

___ supply

___ Supreme Court

___ unconstitutional

___ veto

Explore a Word

Read the paragraph. Think about the meaning of the **bold** word.

> Dalia dreams of being an **entrepreneur**. She plans to go to business school to learn how to set up her own company.

1. What do you think the word means? Write your idea.

   entrepreneur: _____

   _____

2. Write a sentence with the word **entrepreneur**. Show what it means.

   _____

   _____

3. Check the meaning of **entrepreneur** in the Student Dictionary.

4. If your sentence in number 2 above matches the meaning, place a ✓ after it. If your sentence does not match the meaning, write a better sentence.

   _____

   _____

5. Make a simple drawing to show the meaning of **entrepreneur**.

Explore a Word

Read the paragraph. Think about the meaning of the **bold** word. Then, check the Student Dictionary.

> A person, a group, or a region produces certain kinds of products and services. Each trades with others who specialize in different kinds of products and services. **Specialization** is the basis for economic activities of all kinds.

Fill in the chart to show your understanding of specialization.

1. What is specialization?	2. Examples:
3. Why is specialization needed?	**4.** How do people choose or develop specializations?

 Word Alert!

The word *specialization* is made by adding the suffixes *-ize* and *-ation* to the base word *special*. Can you think of two other words that end with these suffixes? (Hint: Start by thinking of words that end with *-ize*.)

Compare Words

Read the paragraph. Think about the meaning of each **bold** word. Then, check the Student Dictionary.

> The next time you visit a supermarket, think about where all of the products have come from. Farmers and manufacturers around the world need methods of **distribution** to deliver their products to thousands of stores. Customers' **consumption** of products keeps the stores in business.

Read each description. Is it an example of distribution or consumption? Circle the answer.

1. Every day, trucks carrying milk leave dairy farms.   distribution   consumption

2. A container ship carries thousands of tons of cargo across the ocean.   distribution   consumption

3. Children choose stuffed animals at a toy store.   distribution   consumption

4. Gasoline is pumped into the underground tanks of a filling station.   distribution   consumption

5. A car pulls up to a filling station for gasoline.   distribution   consumption

6. Government reports say that people are spending less in stores.   distribution   consumption

7. More customers visit a furniture store while a sale is on.   distribution   consumption

8. Automobile manufacturers decide where to send their cars.   distribution   consumption

Compare Words

Read the paragraph. Think about the meaning of each **bold** word. Then, check the Student Dictionary.

> Prices for goods are often determined by the law of **supply** and **demand**. A price can depend on how many people want the item and how many are available. When the demand is high and the supply is low, the price will be high. When the supply is high and the demand is low, the price will be lower.

Fill in the chart by writing **high** or **low** under *Supply* and *Demand*. Think about it. Then, write **high** or **low** under *Price*.

Item	Supply	Demand	Price
1. tickets to a rock concert			
2. friendship bracelets			
3. autographed photo of a movie star			
4. broccoli			
5. movie tickets			
6. diamond earrings			
7. new, popular computer game			
8. baseball cap			
9. newest model cell phone			
10. chewing gum			

Compare Words

Read the paragraph. Think about the meaning of each **bold** word. Then, check the Student Dictionary.

> The First **Amendment** to the US Constitution guarantees Americans freedom to worship as they wish, freedom of speech, and freedom of the press. It also guarantees the right to peaceful **assembly** and the right to **petition** the government.

Complete each sentence with one or more words that make sense.

1. In a country with freedom of assembly, people _____ to protest their government's actions.

2. A petition is a _____ that people sign.

3. One reason that citizens sign a petition is to _____ lawmakers to vote for or against a bill.

4. People who wish to exercise their right of assembly must _____ _____ their local government.

5. In some countries, governments do not permit assembly. In these countries, the people _____ to express their views.

6. An _____ is an addition or a change to the US Constitution. The first 10 are called the Bill of Rights.

Complete each statement with your own idea.

7. There are limits to the right of assembly, especially if _____

   _____ .

8. More than 100 students signed a petition to the principal because they _____

   _____ .

Compare Words

Read the paragraphs. Think about the meaning of each **bold** term. Then, check the Student Dictionary.

> Lawmakers vote on a bill to decide if it will become a law. If there are 100 lawmakers, at least 51 of them must vote for the bill if it is to pass. Lawmakers follow the democratic principle of **majority rule**.
>
> Another principle in a democracy is fairness. Two amendments to the US Constitution forbid a government from depriving a person of "life, liberty, or property, without **due process** of law."

Read the questions. Use your answers to fill in the chart. Then, add more details to the chart.

- What is the purpose of both majority rule and due process?
- What do majority rule and due process have to do with laws?
- How does majority rule work?
- What is fair about majority rule? What is unfair about it?
- What does due process have to do with people accused of crimes?
- What are some actions that show due process?

majority rule	both	due process

Make Connections

Read the paragraph. Think about the meaning of each **bold** term. Then, check the Student Dictionary.

> As the toy moved from one station of the **assembly line** to the next, workers added or checked its parts. **Mass production** was possible because each toy had identical parts.

Underline the better ending to each sentence.

1. Mass production takes place
   A. in factories.   B. outdoors.

2. An assembly line is used to produce
   A. a computer.   B. a one-of-a-kind artwork.

3. Each job on an assembly line is usually done
   A. quickly.   B. slowly.

4. Many assembly lines use
   A. large rooms filled with computer operators.
   B. computer-operated machines called *robots*.

5. The mass production of TVs means that
   A. many workers make one complete set.
   B. one worker makes one complete set.

6. As a result of mass production, goods often become
   A. better in quality.   B. lower in price.

 # Look It Up!

Each meaning of a word is numbered in a dictionary entry. Look up the word *assembly* in a classroom dictionary. Write a brief meaning that fits with each phrase below.

7. the right to peaceful assembly:_____

8. lawmakers in the state assembly: _____

9. the assembly of parts: _____

Name _____

Make Connections

Read the paragraph. Think about the meaning of each **bold** term. Then, check the Student Dictionary.

> Voters elect lawmakers to the two houses of the US **Congress**. The **Senate** has 100 members, made up of two senators from each state. The **House of Representatives**, or the House, has 435 members. The number of representatives from each state depends on the population of that state.

Circle *Yes* or *No* for each question. Write your reason on the line.

1. Is Congress part of the US Senate? Yes No

_____

2. Are more lawmakers in the House than in the Senate? Yes No

_____

3. Do the lawmakers in the Senate represent voters? Yes No

_____

4. Could a state have more senators than representatives in Congress? Yes No

_____

5. Could a senator vote in the House? Yes No

_____

 Word Alert!

Read the two-word term below. Underline the base word in each of the words. Then, use those base words to explain what the term means.

congressional representation

_____

_____

Name _____

Make Connections

Read the paragraphs. Think about the meaning of each **bold** term. Then, check the Student Dictionary.

> As the chief of the **executive** branch, the US president appoints many **officials** to positions in the government. The president also nominates justices to the **Supreme Court**, the highest court in the **judicial** system.
>
> Only Congress has the power to pass laws, but a system of **checks and balances** means that the executive branch and the judicial branch can limit Congress's power. The president may **veto** a bill by refusing to sign it and sending it back to Congress. The Supreme Court can declare a law **unconstitutional**.

Complete each sentence with one or more words that make sense.

1. Because of checks and balances, each of the three main branches of government _____ the others.

2. The executive branch includes departments in which officials _____ _____ that laws are enforced.

3. When the Supreme Court says that a state law is unconstitutional, it is saying that the state has _____ that breaks the law of the land.

4. The judicial branch includes judges who _____ in federal courts.

5. Congress can still pass a bill that the president has vetoed if at least two-thirds of _____ in each house vote to override the veto.

 Word Alert!

The word *unconstitutional* is made of the prefix *un-* and the word *constitutional*. The prefix *un-* means "not." What does *constitutional* mean?

_____

Academic Vocabulary Practice • Grade 5 • CD-104810

Play with Words

Code Words

Choose the word or words that complete each sentence. Circle the letter.

1. A conveyor belt moves products along ___.
   a an assembly line
   b distribution
   c checks and balances

2. The Supreme Court is in the ___ branch.
   r executive
   s judicial
   t Senate

3. The Senate is part of ___.
   s Congress
   t the House of Representatives
   u the Supreme Court

4. Prices for goods are usually decided by supply and ___.
   d petition
   e demand
   f specialization

5. Companies that make the same products are in ___.
   q consumption
   r mass production
   m competition

6. Three branches of government share power with ___.
   a majority rule
   b checks and balances
   c mass production

7. The US president can sign or ___ a bill.
   k petition
   l veto
   m unconstitutional

8. Officials may be elected with ___.
   w due process
   x specialization
   y majority rule

Write the circled letters in order to find the name of a right that belongs to citizens in a democracy.

_____

Play with Words

Synonym Pairs

Read each clue. Find and circle the two synonyms that match the clue.

1. unconstitutional   w i l l e g a l h a u n l a w f u l t

2. specialization   s h j o b o u p r o f e s s i o n l

3. a judicial matter   d y o t r i a l u a c a s e l w a

4. lawmaking body   y s l e g i s l a t u r e k e c o n g r e s s

5. distribution   e p a d e l i v e r y f t t r a n s p o r t e r y o

6. the buying of goods   u g c o n s u m p t i o n i s p e n d i n g

7. need   v e d e m a n d i t i n t e r e s t t o s

8. businessperson   o m e e n t r e p r e n e u r o n b o s s

9. request   e e l p e t i t i o n s e a d d r e s s y

10. assembly   o u r g a t h e r i n g w o r a l l y r d

Look back to find the letters you did NOT circle. Write them in order to find a riddle and its answer.

___ ___ ___ ___   ___ ___ ___ ___ ___   ___ ___ ___   ___ ___ ___ ___ ___ ___

___ ___ ___ ___   ___ ___ ___ ___ ___   ___ ___ ___   ___ ___ ___ ___

___ ___   ___ ___   ___ ___ ___ ___ ___ ___ ___   ___ ___ ___ ___?

(___ ___ ___ ___   ___ ___ ___ ___)

Important Art
Words You Need to Know

Use this list to keep track of how well you know the new words.

0 = Don't Know   1 = Know Somewhat   2 = Know Well

___ abstract

___ ceramics

___ choreographer

___ color wheel

___ comedy

___ complementary colors

___ depict

___ dialogue

___ glaze

___ graphic design

___ harmony

___ illusion

___ kiln

___ layout

___ monologue

___ opera

___ perspective

___ pigment

___ primary colors

___ proportion

___ secondary colors

___ symphony

___ texture

___ tragedy

___ vanishing point

Explore a Word

Read the paragraph. Think about the meaning of the **bold** word.

> The members of a chorus learn to sing in **harmony** with one another. Painters and other artists put parts together to create harmony in their artwork. Harmony is pleasing to hear and see.

1. What do you think the word means? Write your idea.

   harmony: _____

   _____

2. Write a sentence with the word **harmony**. Show what it means.

   _____

   _____

3. Check the meaning of **harmony** in the Student Dictionary.

4. If your sentence in number 2 above matches the meaning, place a ✓ after it. If your sentence does not match the meaning, write a better sentence.

   _____

   _____

5. Make a simple drawing to show the meaning of **harmony**.

Explore a Word

Read the sentence. Think about the meaning of the **bold** word. Then, check the Student Dictionary.

> The dancers learned the steps that the **choreographer** arranged.

Fill in the chart to show your understanding of a choreographer's work.

I. What does a choreographer do?	**2.** How are choreographers trained?
3. What must a choreographer think about?	**4.** Where do choreographers work?

🔍 Look It Up!

The words *choreographer*, *choreograph*, and *choreography* share Greek word forms. What are those forms? Use a classroom dictionary to look up the words and tell about their origins. Complete each statement below.

5. The Greek word part *choreo* means _____.

6. The Greek word part *graph* means _____.

Compare Words

Read the paragraph. Think about the meaning of each **bold** word. Then, check the Student Dictionary.

> Two main kinds of drama are **comedy** and **tragedy**. The great playwright William Shakespeare wrote both kinds of plays. In his comedies, he used wit and humor to amuse audiences. In his tragedies, he used serious events to stir deep emotion from audiences.

Read the description of each play by William Shakespeare. Is it a comedy or a tragedy? Circle the answer.

1. In *Romeo and Juliet*, the fighting between two
    families leads to the death of two young people in love.   comedy   tragedy

2. One of the most famous scenes in drama comes
    from *Macbeth*, in which a cruel queen goes mad
    because of the deaths she has caused.   comedy   tragedy

3. In *A Midsummer Night's Dream*, the mischievous
    Puck sprinkles love potion on characters and
    causes a big mix-up.   comedy   tragedy

4. In *Twelfth Night*, a young woman disguised as
    a boy falls in love with a man. This man loves a
    woman who falls in love with the boy.   comedy   tragedy

5. *Hamlet* tells the story of a young prince who
    wants to avenge his father's death by destroying
    his father's murderer, the new king.   comedy   tragedy

6. Would you prefer to see a comedy or a tragedy? Explain.

    _____

    _____

Compare Words

Read the paragraph. Think about the meaning of each **bold** word. Then, check the Student Dictionary.

> We listened to the orchestra play the famous *Jupiter* **symphony** by the composer Mozart. After that work, we heard music from Mozart's **opera** *The Marriage of Figaro*.

Write the word *opera* (or *operas*) and *symphony* (or *symphonies*) to complete each pair of sentences.

1. _____ are long musical works for an orchestra.
_____ are works of drama in which actors sing their lines.

2. In the 1700s, Italian _____ were performed with musical introductions called *overtures*. Composers began to change overtures into longer works that became known as _____.

3. Austrian composer Wolfgang Amadeus Mozart wrote more than 600 works. His longer works for orchestra are called classical _____. His _____ are famous for combining the feelings of characters with music that conveys those feelings.

4. The stories used for _____ are about love, betrayal, and powerful emotions. _____ often suggest emotions, but they do not usually tell stories.

5. _____ are theatrical performances with stage sets, costumes, dancing, and an orchestra hidden from the audience's view. _____ are played on the stage of a concert hall by the musicians of an orchestra.

6. The German composer Ludwig van Beethoven wrote some of the best-known _____ played today. He also wrote many vocal works, including the _____ *Fidelio*.

Compare Words

Read the paragraph. Think about the meaning of each **bold** word. Then, check the Student Dictionary.

> The play's **dialogue** included a section in which five characters were talking at once. Suddenly, one of the actors stepped to the front of the stage to deliver a **monologue**.

Circle the word that completes each sentence.

1. Read the script to find the words of (dialogue/monologue) after each character's name.

2. One of the most famous (dialogues/monologues) in a play is Hamlet's "To Be or Not to Be" speech.

3. An actor who delivers a (dialogue/monologue) shows that character's thoughts and feelings.

4. Two characters had a fast and funny (dialogue/monologue) in the second act.

5. Actors memorize their lines and try to make the (dialogue/monologue) sound like natural conversation.

6. The playwright included a (dialogue/monologue) for one of the minor characters in the play.

 Word Alert!

The prefix *mono-* means "one." Answer the question with your own ideas.

Why should an actor not use a monotone in a monologue?

_____

_____

Name _____

Make Connections

Look at the pictures and read the caption. Think about the meaning of each **bold** word. Then, check the Student Dictionary.

Some artworks clearly **depict** people and things. Other artworks are made in an **abstract** style, with elements that are not realistic.

Follow each instruction.

1. Think of a statue you have seen in a public place. Tell what the statue depicts.

   _____

2. Explain the difference between depicting a scene and picturing a scene.

   _____

   _____

3. An abstract painting has the title *Action*. What might it show?

   _____

   _____

4. Depict a face in an abstract way.

 Challenge!

Find a book about art. Choose an example of an abstract piece of artwork. Prepare a short talk to explain what the artist has depicted and what makes the work abstract.

Make Connections

Read the paragraph. Think about the meaning of each **bold** word. Then, check the Student Dictionary.

> The art of **ceramics** is one of the oldest crafts in the world. Special clay is dug from the earth and shaped into a pot or other form. A coating of **glaze**, made from colored minerals and water, is added. Then, the ceramic clay is baked in a **kiln**.

Complete each sentence with one or more words that make sense.

1. The colored minerals in the glaze melt from the _____ in the kiln.

2. Ceramic objects include pots, figures of animals, and _____.

3. The glassy _____ of a ceramic object is the result of the glaze.

4. A ceramic object is "fired" in a _____ , where temperatures are high.

5. Ceramic pots were practical items, but they were also _____.

6. The kind of pottery called *china* was invented in ancient China, a land with a long _____ of ceramic arts.

7. Ceramic sculptures are shaped from _____.

8. Ceramic artists test different substances in clay and glazes. In many ways, ceramic artists are like _____ , because both experiment with natural substances.

Make Connections

Read the paragraph. Think about the meaning of each **bold** word. Then, check the Student Dictionary.

> Have you ever made a poster to show information? How did you decide where to position the text and the art in your **layout**? How did you decide on the sizes and the shapes of words and pictures so that everything would be in **proportion**? Your decisions had to do with a field of art called **graphic design**.

Underline the correct ending to each sentence.

1. You can see examples of graphic design in
   A. a magazine.   B. a musical performance.

2. You can see examples of layouts on
   A. restaurant tables.   B. restaurant menus.

3. The designer of a Web page plans the proportions of
   A. sounds.   B. images.

4. If the elements on a page are out of proportion,
   A. the page looks out of balance.
   B. the page looks boring.

5. A graphic designer makes a layout to plan
   A. a photograph.   B. a sign in a store.

6. One job in graphic design is
   A. making or choosing typefaces.
   B. planning the layout of a room.

Make Connections

Read the paragraph. Think about the meaning of each **bold** word. Then, check the Student Dictionary.

Artists use techniques of **perspective** to make a flat surface seem three-dimensional. For example, an artist might create the **illusion** of distance with lines that meet in a **vanishing point**. Artists also use shading and lines to create the illusion of softness, roughness, or other **textures**.

Look at the picture. Use the vocabulary words to create captions that point out different elements.

Make Connections

Read the paragraph. Think about the meaning of each **bold** word. Then, check the Student Dictionary.

> Artists work with colors that come from **pigments** in sources such as paints and inks. The **primary colors** in pigments are red, yellow, and blue. An equal mixture of two primary colors makes **secondary colors**. Colors arranged on a **color wheel** show relationships. Artists may choose complementary colors to create strong contrasts. **Complementary colors** are on opposite sides of the color wheel.

Use colored pencils, markers, or paints to fill in the color wheel. Use the five vocabulary words described above to write captions for it.

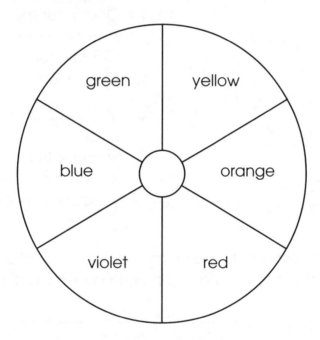

⭐ Challenge!

Think about the meanings of *primary* and *secondary*, and where primary and secondary colors are on the color wheel. What is the category for the colors yellow-orange, red-orange, red-violet, blue-violet, blue-green, and yellow-green? Where would they go on the color wheel? Do research to check your ideas. Write the answers below.

_____

_____

Play with Words

Code Words

Choose the word or words that complete each sentence. Circle the letter.

1. Carvings on a ceramic vase give it ___.
   a texture
   b pigment
   c glaze

2. The strings in the symphony orchestra played in ___.
   q opera
   r harmony
   s abstract

3. The stage scenery ___ a forest.
   r layout
   s illusion
   t depicts

4. Red is a ___.
   g graphic design
   h secondary color
   i primary color

5. A ___ is like an oven.
   s kiln
   t pigment
   u glaze

6. The eyes on the portrait look odd because they are not in ___.
   s complementary colors
   t proportion
   u vanishing point

7. One actor spoke a ___.
   r monologue
   s dialogue
   t comedy

8. Mix equal amounts of primary colors to get ___.
   w complementary colors
   x a color wheel
   y secondary colors

Write the circled letters in order to find a word that names what is shown by a musician, choreographer, singer, dancer, sculptor, painter, or anyone in a creative field.

_____

Play with Words

Words and Clues

Find the clues that match the vocabulary words. Write the letter of the correct clue in each blank.

Clues

1. complementary colors ___   **F** orange and violet, for example

2. dialogue ___   **R** the opposite of tragedy

3. ceramics ___   **T** blue and orange, for example

4. vanishing point ___   **Y** a potter's craft

5. comedy ___   **L** a source of color

6. graphic design ___   **H** silky or bumpy, for example

7. symphony ___   **E** words in a script

8. texture ___   **C** *Beethoven's Ninth*, for example

9. pigment ___   **N** a meeting place for imaginary lines

10. secondary colors ___   **I** the art of text and art

Write the letters in order to find an answer to this question: *Why are the arts valuable?*

___ H ___ ___   E ___ ___ ___ ___ ___   ___ I ___ E!

Game Ideas and Suggestions

Use games and activities to help students better hear, see, and remember content-area vocabulary words. The suggestions on these pages can be used with the words in this book and with any other vocabulary words that students are learning.

Charades

Choose about 10 vocabulary words. Write the words on slips of paper and display them. Give students time to think about the words before removing the slips. Then, divide the class into two teams. One team member chooses a slip, holds up fingers to indicate the number of syllables, and pantomimes the word. Teammates try to guess the word within a certain time limit.

Word Art

Help students select vocabulary words to depict as art. Encourage them to use letter shapes and arrangements to indicate what the words mean. Prompt students with questions such as "How might you draw the letters of the word *refraction*?", "Could you position the words *latitude* and *longitude* to show their relationship?", or "What might happen to the letters in *secede*?"

Vocabulary Bingo

Reproduce and distribute the Vocabulary Bingo game card on page 106 for each student. Display a list of 40 vocabulary words and have each student choose 25 words to write on his card. Write each of the 40 words on a separate slip of paper. Shuffle the slips and choose one slip at a time. Instead of reading the word aloud, offer a clue about it. For example, for the word *consumption*, you might suggest the content area: "This is an economics term having to do with buying and selling." Or, use a strong context sentence with "blank" for the word: "Drivers are looking for ways to reduce their 'blank' of gasoline." Students should check off the word if it is on their grids. The first student to complete four across, down, or diagonally says "Bingo" and reads aloud the four words.

Hink-Pinks

A *hink-pink* is a pair of rhyming words that answer a silly riddle. A *hinky-pinky* is a two-syllable pair. Use vocabulary words in the riddle and have students, individually or in pairs, come up with the hink-pink reply. Encourage students to review their vocabulary lists and write their own hink-pink riddles for classmates. Examples of riddles:

• What do you call a rabbit in a *comedy*? (a funny bunny)

• What do you call a dog outside in 100% *humidity*? (a wet pet)

• What do you call a *myth* with no women characters? (a male tale)

Card Pairs

Use index cards cut in half to prepare a deck of 52 cards. Write 26 vocabulary words and 26 synonyms or short definitions on the cards. The cards can be used in a variety of

Game Ideas and Suggestions

games, such as Memory or Concentration. Here is one suggestion:

- **Go Fish!** for 2 to 5 Players
- Each player is dealt five cards. The remaining cards are placed facedown in a pile.
- The player to the right of the dealer starts by setting aside any pairs. Then, she asks the player on the right for a card needed to make a pair. "Do you have *foreshadowing*?" or "Do you have the meaning of *foreshadowing*?"
- If the holder has the requested card, he hands it over. If the holder does not have it, the player must "go fish" and draw the top card from the pile. If the player cannot make a match, the next player takes a turn.
- The winner is the first player with no cards in hand or the player with the most pairs after all cards have been drawn.

Word Hunt

Emphasize that vocabulary words appear in print and online in a variety of informational resources. As you come across a vocabulary word—in a headline, a news article, an advertisement, or another resource—save the printed source or make a printout. Challenge students to read the text to find the vocabulary word and to explain what it means in the provided context.

Dictionary Guess

Have one student randomly choose a word from the Student Dictionary and read the definition aloud to the class. Partners or small groups then try to write the vocabulary word that matches the definition. Continue until each student has had a chance to choose a word and read its definition aloud. Award a point for each correct word.

Racetrack Games

Have students design their own racetrack board games or make one from a template you provide, such as the template on page 107. Here is one way to use the template.

- Select 25 vocabulary words for students to write in the spaces.
- Make a small cardboard spinner by drawing a circle divided into three sections labeled 1, 2, and 3. The "spinner" can be a paper clip attached to a paper fastener.
- Provide small objects for students to use as markers.
- Each player spins, and the player with the highest number goes first.
- The player spins and moves the marker the number of spaces shown. The player must say the word on the space and demonstrate knowledge of it by giving its definition or using it in a good context sentence.
- Players may use a dictionary to check the player's response. A player who is not correct loses a turn.
- The first player to reach the finish line wins.

B	I	N	G	O

Academic Vocabulary Practice • Grade 5 • CD-104810

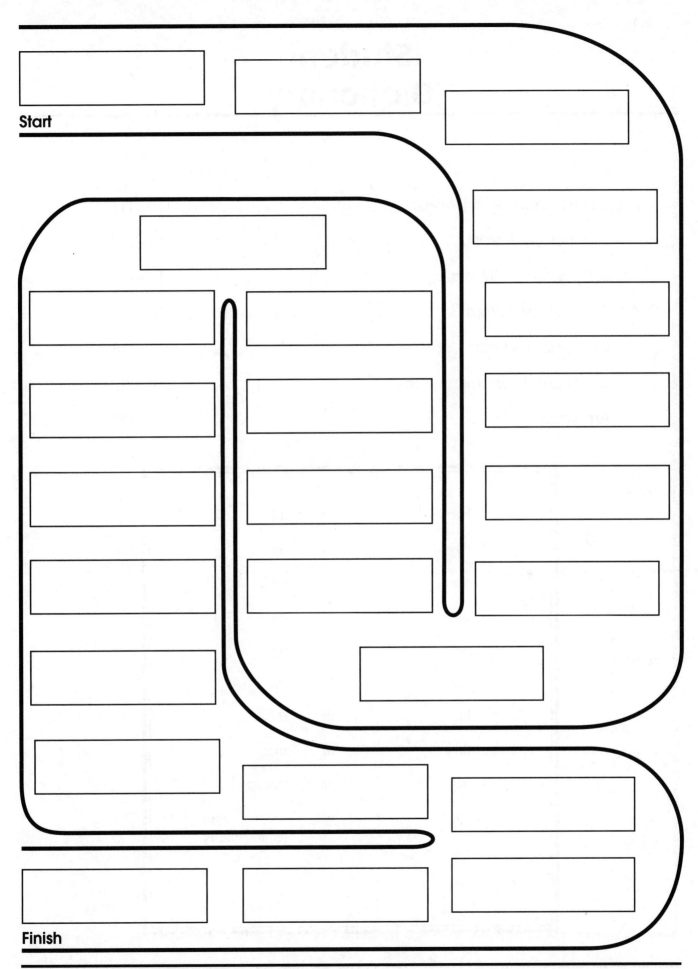

Start

Finish

Student
Dictionary

a	bat	oi	**oil**
ā	day	o͞o	**too**
â	share	o͝o	took
ä	father	ou	**out**
e	net	u	**up**
ē	me	û	fur
i	big	th	**th**ink
ī	time	*th*	**th**at
o	hot	zh	treasure
ō	go	ə	happen, robin, lemon, circus
ô	for		
ȯ	saw		

 Academic Vocabulary Practice • Grade 5 • CD-104810

Important Math Words I Need to Know

acute angle (ə kyo͞ot' ān' gəl) *noun* An angle of less than 90 degrees.

algebra (al' jə brə) *noun* The branch of mathematics in which numerical relationships are shown with a combination of numbers and letters that stand for numbers.

average (av' rij) *noun* The sum of a set of numbers divided by the number of items in the set; the mean of a set of numbers. *For example, the average of six numbers is the sum of those numbers divided by 6.*

circumference (sə(r) 'kəm(p) fər en(t)s) *noun* The outer boundary of a figure or area, especially a circle.

composite (käm 'pä zət) *adjective* Describes a number that can be factored into two or more prime factors, not counting 1 or itself.

coordinates (kō ôr' di nits) *noun* A pair of numbers used to locate a point on a grid or a graph.

data (dā' tə or dat'ə) *noun* Facts and numbers that are gathered and used to find patterns.

degree (di grē') *noun* A unit used to measure angles, equal to $\frac{1}{360}$ of a full circle.

divisible (di viz' ə bəl) *adjective* Able to be divided by a number without a remainder. *12 is divisible by 12, 1, 3, 4, 6, and 2.*

equation (i 'kwā zhən) *noun* A number sentence showing two equal mathematical expressions.

expression (ik 'spresh ən) *noun* Numbers and symbols grouped together to show a mathematical value.

formula (fôr' myə lə) *noun* A mathematical statement of a relationship in which letters and symbols stand for numbers.

frequency (frē' kwən sē) *noun* **1.** The number of times an event occurs in a period of time. **2.** The number of times an event occurs within a group.

integer (in'tə jər) *noun* A positive or negative whole number or zero.

isosceles triangle (ī sos' ə lēz' trī' ān' gəl) *noun* A triangle in which two of the three sides are of equal length.

mean (mēn) *noun* The leveling of a set of numbers by decreasing the larger numbers and increasing the smaller numbers; the average. The mean is found by adding the numbers and dividing by the number of them. *For example, the average of six numbers is the sum of those numbers divided by 6.*

median (mē' dē ən) *noun* The middle number in a set of numbers that are arranged in order of value. The median of a set of even numbers is the mean of the two middle numbers (the sum of the two numbers divided by 2).

mode (mōd) *noun* The number appearing most frequently in a set of data.

negative integer (neg' ə tiv in' tə jər) *noun* A whole number that is less than zero. Negative integers are written as –1, –2, –3, and so on.

obtuse angle (ob to͞os ān' gəl) *noun* An angle greater than 90 degrees and less than 180 degrees.

prime (prīm) *noun, adjective* A number, not including zero, which is divisible only by itself and 1. *The largest 3-digit prime number is 997.*

ratio (rā' shē ō) *noun* The relationship between two numbers or amounts. A ratio is often expressed as a fraction or with the word *to*. *Example: a ratio of $\frac{2}{3}$ or 2 to 3.*

sample (sam' pəl) *noun* A group chosen to represent the whole in a data collection. Most samples are chosen at random.

scalene triangle (skā' lēn' trī' ān' gəl) *noun* A triangle with three sides of different lengths.

square ('skwer) *noun* A number that is a result of multiplying one number by itself.

vertex (vûr' teks) *noun* The meeting point of two rays of an angle, two sides of a plane figure, or at least three sides of a solid figure.

Important Science and Health Words I Need to Know

air pressure (âr presh' ər) *noun* The downward push caused by the weight of the air surrounding Earth. *Air pressure is greatest at sea level.*

anther ('an(t) thər) *noun* The part of a flower that produces and contains pollen. The anther and the filament make up the stamen.

atmosphere (at' mə sfēr') *noun* The air surrounding Earth, held in place by Earth's gravity. *The gases nitrogen and oxygen make up most of the atmosphere.*

atom (at' əm) *noun* The basic unit of matter. The atom is the smallest unit of an element. An atom is made of a positively charged center (nucleus) surrounded by negatively charged electrons.

carbon dioxide (kâr' bən dī ok' sīd) *noun* A colorless and odorless gas, formed from a chemical bond between atoms of carbon and oxygen, CO_2. *Plants take in carbon dioxide, and people breathe out carbon dioxide.*

chlorophyll (klôr 'ə fil) *noun* The colored substance, usually green, found in plant cells. It enables the cells to capture light energy and use the energy in photosynthesis.

compound (kom 'pound') *noun* A substance made of atoms of two or more elements. Unlike a mixture, a compound is formed with chemical bonds. *Water is a compound of the elements oxygen and hydrogen.*

conclusion (kən klōō' zhən) *noun* A decision or judgment based on careful study of data along with logical reasoning.

conduction (kən 'dək shən) *noun* The process of transferring something, such as heat, from one point to another through a solid item.

convection (kən 'vek shən) *noun* The motion in which warm parts rise and colder parts sink.

electromagnetic spectrum (i lek' trō mag net' ik spek' trəm) *noun* The range of waves of electric and magnetic energy, or electromagnetic radiation. The waves travel at the same speed but at different frequencies. At the lowest frequencies (longest wavelengths) of the electromagnetic spectrum are gamma rays; at the highest frequencies (shortest wavelengths) are radio waves. Visible light is at the middle range.

electron (i lek' tron') *noun* A tiny particle that has a negative charge and whirls around the nucleus of its atom.

element (el' ə mənt) *noun* A substance made of atoms that have the same number of protons in the nucleus. The periodic table of the elements groups the known elements in order of the number of protons (atomic number). There are more than 100 elements. *Examples of elements are hydrogen, iron, and carbon.*

filament ('fil ə mənt) *noun* A part of a flower. It is the stalk of the stamen and holds the anther.

hypothesis (hī poth' ə sis) *noun* A possible explanation of related facts or observed patterns, which is tested in the form of a scientific investigation.

igneous ('ig nə əs) *adjective* A kind of rock formed by the cooling and hardening of hot magma. It is formed above or below Earth's surface.

lens (lenz) *noun* A piece of glass or other transparent material that has been shaped with curves that bend, or refract, light. *An eyeglass lens is designed to redirect rays of light so that they focus sharply on the back of the eye.*

ligament (lig' ə mənt) *noun* A band of tough fibers of tissue connecting bones at a joint.

metamorphic (met ə 'mor fik) *adjective* A kind of rock formed over time by extreme pressure and heat.

molecule ('mol 'ə kyōōl') *noun* The smallest particle, containing at least two atoms, that makes up a substance.

Important Science and Health Words I Need to Know

motor (mō' tər) *adjective* Of nerves that carry signals from the brain and the spinal cord to the muscles, enabling movement.

nerve (nûrv) *noun* A bundle of fibers through which impulses travel to connect all parts of the body with the spinal cord and the brain.

neuron (nŏŏr' on') *noun* A cell of a nerve, the spinal cord, or the brain that carries velectrical impulses.

opaque (o pāk') *adjective* Not allowing light to pass through. *Tomato juice is an opaque liquid.*

ovary ('ō və rē) *noun* The part of a flower in which seeds form.

petal ('pet əl) *noun* One of the usually brightly colored parts of a flower.

photosynthesis (fō' tō sin' thə sis) *noun* The process used by green plants to make food. Plants use sunlight as the energy source that powers a chemical reaction between water and carbon dioxide, which results in sugar.

prism (priz' m) *noun* A triangular solid, usually made of transparent glass, through which light can be broken into its component colors.

radiation (rād ē 'ā shən) *noun* The process of giving off radiant energy in waves.

reflection (ri flek' shən) *noun* The bouncing back of light rays from a surface.

refraction (ri frak' shən) *noun* The bending of light rays as they pass through one substance and into another, such as from air to water.

sedimentary (sed ə 'men tə rē) *adjective* A kind of rock, formed over time from deposits of sediment.

sensory (sens' ə rē) *adjective* Of nerves that carry signals from sense organs to the spinal cord and brain, providing information about sight, sound, taste, smell, and touch.

sepal ('sēp l) *noun* The usually green leaves at the base of a flower.

spinal cord (spī' nəl kôrd) *noun* The thick cord of nerve tissue that extends from the lowest part of the brain down the spine. Pairs of nerves connect the spinal cord to all parts of the body.

stamen (stā' mən) *noun* The male organ of a flower. The stamen is made of two parts: the anther, which holds pollen, and the filament.

stigma ('stig mə) *noun* The upper part of ta flower's pistil on which pollen grains grow.

style (stī(ə)l) *noun* The long, narrow middle part of a flower's pistil.

tendon (ten' dən) *noun* A band of strong tissue that connects the end of a muscle to a bone.

tissue ('tish ü) *noun* A group of cells in an animal or plant body that are like each other and carry out a job in the body.

translucent (tranz' lōō' sənt) *adjective* Allowing light rays to pass through, but changing their directions. *Objects viewed through translucent glass are blurry.*

transparent (trans' pâr' ənt) *adjective* Allowing light rays to pass through. *Clear glass is transparent.*

vertebrae (vûr' tə brā or vûr' tə brē) *plural noun* The bones that form the spinal column. *singular noun*: vertebra

visible light (viz'ə bəl līt) *noun* The segment of wavelengths of the electromagnetic spectrum that human eyes can detect. Visible light is also called *white light*, and it can be broken into the colors red, orange, yellow, green, blue, bluish purple, and violet.

wavelength ('wāv len(k)th) *noun* The distance between two peaks of a wave.

Important Technology Words I Need to Know

convert (kən vûrt') *verb* To change energy from one form to another. *Our bodies convert the chemical energy in food into the mechanical energy used by our muscles.*

database (dā' tə bās or dat' ə bās) *noun* An arrangement of pieces of information, ordered so that each piece of data can be searched for and retrieved easily. *A table of information is a simple database.*

design process (di zīn' pros' es') *noun* A series of steps that guides engineers in solving problems. Identifying needs and goals, brainstorming solutions, making plans, building, evaluating, and improving are some of the steps in the design process.

digital (dij' i təl) *adjective* Having to do with computers and other devices that work with information represented by numbers.

friction ('frik shən) *noun* What happens when one thing rubs against another.

generator (jen' ə rā' tər) *noun* A machine that converts mechanical energy into electrical energy. A generator works on the principle that movement between a magnet and a circuit of wires produces an electric current.

hydroelectric (hī' drō i lek' trik) *adjective* Having to do with electricity made by converting the energy of running water.

inertia (i nûr' shə) *noun* The property of a body at rest to remain at rest unless a force acts on it, and to keep moving in a straight line unless a force acts on it.

interface (in' tər fās) *noun* The boundary shared by two devices that work together, or the boundary between a human user and a device. *A person can quickly figure out how to use a touch screen if the interface is organized clearly.*

kinetic energy (kə net' ik en' ər jē) *noun* Energy of motion. *Atoms and molecules in motion produce heat, which is a form of kinetic energy.*

network (net' wûrk) *noun* Two or more computers connected directly with cables or connected wirelessly.

potential energy (pə ten' shəl en'ər jē) *noun* Stored energy or energy of position. *An apple dangling from a tree branch has potential energy in the form of its stored chemical energy. It also has potential energy because of its high position, which gravity will act on.*

prototype (prō' tə tīp') *noun* A first, full-size working model of a new product.

receiver (ri sē' vûr) *noun* The part of a device that receives incoming electronic signals and converts them to recognizable forms, such as sound and pictures. *Telephones, televisions, and radios are some devices with receivers.*

satellite (sat' ə līt) *noun* An object put into orbit around Earth that relays communications signals and sends data to Earth.

spreadsheet (spred' shēt') *noun* A computer program that displays text and numbers in rows and columns. A spreadsheet is used for accounting and other activities requiring calculations.

telecommunications (tel' i kəm yoo' nə kā' shənz) *plural noun* The technologies having to do with sending and receiving sound, pictures, and other information at a distance. *Telecommunications include radio, TV, telephones, and computer networks.*

Important Technology Words I Need to Know

template (tem' plət) *noun* **1.** A pattern that is used to guide the making of identical parts. **2.** A computer document or file that has the format already set and can be used to make new documents with that format.

transmitter (tranz mit' ər) *noun* The part of a device that sends outgoing electronic signals. *Telephones have transmitters.*

troubleshooting (trub' əl shoot ing) *noun* The finding and solving of problems in mechanical or electronic systems.

turbine (tûr' bin or tûr bin') *noun* A machine that converts the kinetic energy of flowing water into mechanical energy. A turbine has blades or buckets against which the water flows to turn a wheel or rotor.

Vocabulary Notes

_____

_____

_____

_____

_____

_____

_____

_____

_____

_____

_____

_____

_____

_____

_____

_____

Important Language Arts Words I Need to Know

autobiography (ô' tō bī og' rə fē) *noun* The written story of a person's life told by himself or herself.

bias (bī' əs) *noun* An unfairly positive or negative view of a person or thing; a prejudice. A bias is not supported by facts or evidence.

bibliography (bib' lē og' rə fē) *noun* A list of books, articles, and other sources on a topic, or a list of sources used in research on a topic. A bibliography appears at the end of a report or a book.

colon (kō' lən) *noun* A punctuation mark made of two vertical dots (:). A colon is used at the end of a sentence to introduce an example or a list.

comparative (kəm par' ə tiv) *noun, adjective* The form of an adjective or an adverb that is used to compare two things or to make a comparison with the word *than. Examples: John runs <u>faster</u> than Ben and is <u>more athletic</u> than most boys his age.*

conclusion (kən kloo' zhən) *noun* The end of a story, an essay, or other written work. The conclusion of an essay sums up and restates the most important ideas.

connotation (kon ə' tā' shən) *noun* The suggested feelings and mood of a word, additional to its definition. *The advertisement for soap used words with favorable connotations, such as* pure *and* silky-smooth.

drama (drä' mə) *noun* A play performed by actors.

draw conclusions ('drȯ kən 'klü zhəns) *verb* To use information in a story or in the environment to make an assumption.

evaluate (i val' yoō āt') *verb* To review a written work thoughtfully and make judgments about its ideas, organization, and quality.

figurative language (fig 'yər ə tiv lan' gwəj) *noun* An expression or use of words that goes beyond the literal meaning of the words in order to create an effect. *Idioms,* metaphors, similes, and personification are kinds of figurative language. (Also called a figure of speech.)

flashback (flash' bak') *noun* A time shift to an earlier point in a story sequence, provided for background information.

foreshadowing (fôr shad' ō ing) *noun* A hint in a story of events to come. *Example: If I had only known then what I know now, I would never have accepted the invitation.*

generalization (jen' ər ə li zā' shən) *noun* A statement that applies to all or most people or things. A valid generalization is based on facts and likely to be true. A generalization that is too broad is not likely to be true.

genre (zhän' rə) *noun* A category of literature or other art forms. *Fans of the mystery genre will enjoy* The Case of the Missing Case.

helping verb (help' ing vûrb) *noun* A form of a verb that comes before a main verb, usually to create a verb tense. *Example: I had planned to stay, but I think I will go.*

historical fiction (hi stôr' ik əl fik' shən) *noun* A work of an author's imagination set in the past and based on actual events.

interjection (in' tər jek' shən) *noun* A word or a phrase that expresses feeling and stands alone. An interjection is set off with commas within a sentence or set, as if a separate sentence. *Examples: Wow! Ouch! Hello? Goodness me!*

introduction (in' trə duk' shən) *noun* The first paragraph or section of a written work, in which the author prepares the reader for the ideas to come.

irregular verb (i reg' yə lər vûrb) *noun* A verb that has more than one form in different tenses. Most verbs form the past tense and the past participle with the ending *-ed: walk, walked, have walked. Irregular verbs form those parts differently: eat, ate, have eaten; think, thought, have thought.*

Important Language Arts Words I Need to Know

make inferences ('māk 'in f(ə) rən(t) es) *verb* To make logical guesses about what the facts imply. This is often called "reading between the lines."

myth (mith) *noun* A traditional story that features gods, heroes, and supernatural events. The myths of ancient Greece include stories of Hercules, a hero with superhuman strength.

narrative (nar' ə tiv) *noun* A true or fictional story with a beginning, a middle, and an end.

narrator ('na(ə)r āt ər) *noun* The one who tells the story.

personification (pûr son' i fi kā' shən) *noun* A use of figurative language in which the qualities of a person or an animal are given to nonliving things. *Examples: The wind roared, and the rain hammered its fists.*

persuasive essay (pûr swā' siv es' ā) *noun* A short written work in which the author expresses a viewpoint on a topic, offers supporting facts and evidence, and tries to get readers to agree or take action.

point of view (pȯint əv 'vyü) *noun phrase* The perspective from which a story is told.

possessive pronoun (pə zes' iv prō' noun') *noun* A word that stands the name of an owner and expresses ownership. Possessive pronouns may be used as adjectives. *Examples: <u>his</u> clothes, <u>my</u> home, <u>your</u> name.* Possessive pronouns may stand alone. *Examples: The yellow sweater is <u>his</u>, and the white one is <u>mine</u>.*

preposition (prep' ə zish' ən) *noun* A word that shows the relationship between the noun or pronoun that follows it and another word in the sentence. *Examples: We looked <u>under</u> and <u>behind</u> the chair <u>by</u> the wall, but the keys have vanished <u>from</u> their usual spot.*

revision (ri vizh' ən) *noun* The changes and improvements made to the draft of a written work.

science fiction (sī' əns fik' shən) *noun* A work of an author's imagination in which technologies and scientific ideas are important to the setting and the plot. Science fiction often features space travel, time travel, and humans' relationships with machines and computers.

semicolon (sem' ē kō' lən) *noun* A punctuation mark made of a dot with a comma directly below (;). A semicolon separates ideas more strongly than a comma but not as strongly as a period.

superlative (so͞o pûr' lə tiv) *noun, adjective* The form of an adjective or an adverb that is used to compare three or more things. *Examples: John is the <u>fastest</u> runner on the team and the <u>most athletic</u> child in his family.*

tense (tens) *noun* The form of a verb that expresses the time of action. The three basic tenses are past (I *danced*; they *sang*); present (I *am dancing*; they *are singing*); and future (I *will dance*; they *will sing*).

transition (tran zish' ən) *noun* A word, a phrase, or a sentence that connects one idea to another in a piece of writing. *Examples: an additional point, as a result, first of all, afterward.*

verb phrase (vûrb frāz) *noun* One or more helping verbs and a main verb. *Examples: had answered, is calling, can be smiling.*

Important Social Studies Words I Need to Know

abolitionist (ab' ə lish' ə nist) *noun* A person who opposes slavery and works to abolish, or bring an end to, the buying and selling of humans.

aggression (ə gresh' ən) *noun* The act of invading a people's territory or attacking them; a hostile act.

alliance (ə lī' əns) *noun* The joining of different nations or groups in a shared cause.

American Revolution (ə mer' ə kən rev' ə lōō' shən) *noun* The war between Britain and its American colonies (1775–1783), which resulted in the independence of the colonies from Britain and the founding of the United States of America.

Articles of Confederation ('ärt i kəls   əv kən fed ə 'rā shən) *noun* The first agreement made between the original 13 states.

boycott (boi' kot') *noun* A planned and organized refusal to buy from or deal with a particular business, nation, or group. A boycott is a way to express disapproval or demand an action. *verb* To participate in a boycott.

Civil War (siv' əl wôr) *noun* The war in the United States (1861–1865) between the Union forces and the Southern states that had seceded from the Union and formed the Confederacy. (Also called *the War Between the States*.)

colonial (kə lō' nē əl) *adjective* Having to do with a colony or colonies. A colony is a group of people governed by a distant country or a territory that belongs to a distant country. *During the colonial period in American history, Europeans made new lives in the 13 colonies.*

colonization (kol' ə ni zā' shən) *noun* The setting up of a colony in a distant land. A colony is a group of people governed by a distant country or a territory that belongs to a distant country.

compromise (kom' prə mīz') *noun* A settlement between opposing sides in which each side gives up some of its demands. *A compromise between pro-slavery and anti-slavery lawmakers was reached in 1850, but it did not last.* *verb* To reach a compromise.

Congress ('kän grəs) *noun* The main lawmaking body of a nation.

consequences (kon' sə kwen' səz) *plural noun* The effects that follow an event.

Constitution (kän(t) stə 't(y)ü shən) *noun* A document explaining the basic laws and beliefs of a nation.

convention (kən 'ven chən) *noun* A meeting of people with a common goal.

Declaration of Independence (dek lə 'rā shən əv in də 'pen dən(t)s) *noun* A document written in 1776 to explain why the colonies wanted freedom from British rule.

discrimination (dis krim' ə nā' shən) *noun* Treatment based on race, gender, class, or ethnic background. *Because of racial discrimination, African Americans had fewer educational opportunities than white Americans before the Civil Rights movement.*

Dust Bowl (dust bōl) *noun* The vast area of the south-central United States that in the 1930s, suffered drought and windstorms, blowing great clouds of dry topsoil. *Thousands of farm families abandoned their land because no crops could grow in the Dust Bowl.*

era (ē' rə or er' ə) *noun* A period of time known for certain events. *Example: the Revolutionary Era, an era of exploration.*

expedition (eks' pə dish' ən) *noun* A journey of a group of people for a purpose, such as exploring a new region.

Great Depression (grāt di presh' ən) *noun* The period of US history, beginning with the 1929 stock market crash and ending in about 1940, when businesses failed, jobs disappeared, and poverty was a national problem.

Important Social Studies Words I Need to Know

Harlem Renaissance (här'ləm ren' i säns') *noun* The period, during the 1920s, when African American literature and art blossomed, centered in the section of New York City called Harlem. The word *renaissance* is French for "rebirth"; the Renaissance was a period of art and learning in Europe.

Industrial Revolution (in dus' trē əl rev' ə lōo' shən) *noun* The changes in how goods were produced, beginning in the mid-1700s, and resulting from the development of powered machines. During the Industrial Revolution, machines in factories began to replace the skilled workers who made products by hand.

industrialization (in dus' trē əl i zā' shən) *noun* The growth of methods for producing goods; the development of factories.

Mayflower Compact (mā flaü (-ə)r 'kəm pakt) *noun* The 1620 agreement that bound the Pilgrims to certain laws when they arrived in New England.

missionary (mish' ə ner' ē) *noun* A religious worker who is sent to a foreign country to convert the people to a particular religion.

negotiation (ni gō' shē ā' shən) *noun* Talking with others to resolve a dispute and reach an agreement.

New Deal (nōo dēl) *noun* Laws and actions designed to lead the United States out of economic hard times in the 1930s, introduced by President Franklin D. Roosevelt and his advisers.

plantation (plan tā' shən) *noun* A very large farm in the southern United States, especially one that used slave labor before the Civil War. *Cotton was a leading crop on southern plantations.*

Reconstruction (rē' kən struk' shən) *noun* The 10-year period following the end of the Civil War, in which the federal government ruled the states that had seceded from the Union before the war. The federal government made efforts to protect the rights of former slaves during Reconstruction and passed an amendment granting voting rights to African American men.

republic (ri pub' lik) *noun* A form of government in which citizens vote to elect the representatives who will govern them.

revolutionary (rev' ə lōo' shə ner' ē) *adjective* **1.** Having to do with overthrowing a government and creating a new one. **2.** Bringing a great change.

secede (si sēd') *verb* To withdraw from an organization or a group. *Eleven states in the South seceded from the Union.*

sharecropper (shâr' krop' ər) *noun* A farmer who gives a share of the crops to a landlord as rent for the land.

states' rights (stāts rīts) *noun* The political view that the US Constitution gives only limited power to the federal government and gives each state most of the power to govern its own people.

urbanization (ûr' bə ni zā' shən) *noun* The creation or expansion of cities.

Important Geography Words I Need to Know

annexation (an' ik sā' shən) *noun* The act of attaching territory to a country, a state, or another political unit.

arid (ar'id) *adjective* Dry; without enough rainfall to support trees. *Deserts are arid.*

cartographer (kär tog' rə fûr) *noun* A mapmaker.

humidity (hyo͞o mid' i tē) *noun* The amount of moisture in the air.

latitude (lat' i to͞od') *noun* The distance on Earth's surface north or south of the equator, measured in degrees. Lines of latitude run east-west around the globe.

longitude (lonj' i to͞od') *noun* The distance on Earth's surface east or west of an imaginary line called the prime meridian, measured in degrees. Lines of longitude run north-south between the poles.

parallels (par' ə lelz') *plural noun* Imaginary lines that run east-west around the globe; lines of latitude.

physical feature ('fiz i kəl 'fē chər) *noun phrase* A characteristic or aspect of Earth's surface, such as land formation or climate.

political boundary (pə lit' i kəl boun' drē) *noun* The border between countries, states, counties, or other political units.

population density (pop' yə lā' shən dens' i tē) *noun* A measure that tells how crowded with people a particular region is. Population density is expressed as people per square mile or square kilometer.

prime meridian (prīm mə rid' ē ən) *noun* The imaginary line that runs between the North and the South Poles and is a reference for distances east and west. The prime meridian is at 0 degrees and runs through Greenwich, England.

projection (prə jek' shən) *noun* A system that a mapmaker uses to show the curved surface of Earth on a flat surface of a map.

savanna (sə van' ə) *noun* A grassland with wide spaces between trees. Savannas are found in regions that have rainy and dry seasons.

tectonic plates (tek ton' ik plāts) *plural noun* The large, thin, irregularly shaped pieces of Earth's outer layer, which move in relation to each other.

terrain (tə rān') *noun* The ground and its particular features. *The hikers crossed the rugged terrain.*

time zone (tīm zōn) *noun* One of the 24 divisions of the globe, in which the same time is used according to a standard.

tropical (trop' i kəl) *noun* Of the region of Earth's surface that lies between two parallels on either side of the equator. *Some tropical climates are hot, with rainy and dry seasons.*

Important Civics and Economics Words I Need to Know

amendment (ə 'men(d) mənt) *noun* A change in the wording or meaning of a law, a bill, or a motion, especially for the better.

assembly (ə sem' blē) *noun* The gathering of people for a common purpose. *Freedom of assembly is the right to gather for political meetings.*

assembly line (ə sem'blē līn) *noun* A series of stations at which workers put together, or assemble, the parts of a product.

checks and balances (cheks and bal' ən səs) *noun* The spread of powers and responsibilities among the legislative (lawmaking), executive, and judicial branches of the US government. Each branch can check, or hold back, the actions of the others so that all three branches are in balance.

Congress (kong' grəs) *noun* The lawmaking body of the US government, made of the House of Representatives and the Senate.

consumption (kən sump' shən) *noun* The act of using up goods and services by buying them. Consumers' purchases lead to consumption.

demand (di 'mand) *noun* The amount of an item or a service that is wanted at a particular price.

distribution (dis' trə byōo' shən) *noun* The process of supplying goods to stores and other businesses that sell directly to customers.

due process (dōo pros' es') *noun* The steps taken to protect a person's legal rights, especially the rights of someone accused of a crime. (Also called *due process of law.)*

entrepreneur (on' trə prə nûr') *noun* A businessperson who plans, starts, and runs a company.

executive (ig zek' yə tiv) *adjective* Of the branch of government that carries out the law. *The US Attorney General heads the Department of Justice in the executive branch.*

House of Representatives (hous uv rep' ri zen' tə tivz) *noun* The lower house of the US Congress or of most state legislatures. (Also called *the House.)*

judicial (jōo' dish' əl) *adjective* Having to do with judges and judgments in courts of law.

majority rule (mə jôr' i tē rōol) *noun* The practice in which at least one more than half of the group makes a decision for the whole group. *Eleven of the 20 students voted to visit the park, so majority rule meant that the other nine students agreed to visit the park too.*

mass production (mas prə duk' shən) *noun* The making of products in large quantities by standardizing parts and dividing the work into different jobs done by different workers.

official (ə fish' əl) *noun* Someone who holds an office or a position of authority, especially in government. *adjective* Having to do with an office or a department of government or authority. (*an official policy.)*

petition (pə tish' ən) *noun* A formal written document requesting an action from an authority. *verb* To make a request of an authority.

Senate (sen' it) *noun* The upper house of the US Congress or of most state legislatures.

specialization (spesh' ə li zā' shən) *noun* The feature of an economy in which production of goods and services is divided among different sources. *Specialization probably began when early toolmakers exchanged their products for food from hunters.*

supply (se 'plī) *noun* The amount of something that is available at one time.

Supreme Court (sōo prēm' kôrt) *noun* The highest federal court in the United States.

unconstitutional (un' kon sti tōo' shə nəl) *adjective* Not following the ideas laid out in the constitution of a nation or a state.

Important Civics and Economics Words I Need to Know

veto (vē' tō) *noun* **1.** The power of the US president to reject a bill passed by Congress. **2.** The written message from the president to Congress, explaining the reason for the refusal to sign the bill. *verb* To use the power of a veto.

Vocabulary Notes

_____

_____

_____

_____

_____

_____

_____

_____

_____

_____

_____

_____

_____

_____

_____

_____

_____

Important Art Words I Need to Know

abstract (ab' strakt') *adjective* In a style of art that is not realistic.

ceramics (sə ram' iks) *noun* The art of using special clay to shape objects and baking them at high temperatures.

choreographer (kôr' ē og' rə fər) *noun* A person who creates and arranges the steps in a dance to be performed.

color wheel (kul' ər wēl) *noun* A circular chart that shows colors and their relationships. *Designers use color wheels to plan patterns of colors.*

comedy (kom' i dē) *noun* A play or other dramatic work intended to entertain with humor. They usually have happy endings.

complementary colors (kom' plə men' tə rē kul' ərz) *plural noun* Colors such as red and green, which are opposite on a color wheel and provide a strong contrast when next to each other in an artwork. *Mixing an equal mixture of complementary colors produces brown or gray.*

depict (di pikt') *verb* To show in a picture, asculpture, or another artwork. *The painting depicts a busy street.*

dialogue (dī' ə log') *noun* 1. The conversation between characters in a play. 2. The lines in a script that show spoken words.

glaze (glāz) *noun* A coating of material made of water and minerals, which is applied to ceramic clay before firing in a kiln. The glaze forms a thin, glassy surface.

graphic design (graf' ik di zīn') *noun* The art of planning the lettering and the pictures for posters, books, other printed materials, and Web pages.

harmony (här' mə nē) *noun* 1. A combination of parts that makes the whole pleasing to the eye or the ear. 2. In music, the combination of notes in a chord or a combination of sounds that work together well.

illusion (i lo͞o' zhən) *noun* Something that fools the eye. *Painters create the illusion of depth in a flat surface.*

kiln (kil) or (kiln) *noun* An oven that bakes, or fires, ceramics.

layout (lā' out') *noun* 1. The process of arranging type and art on a page. 2. A plan for the elements of a finished artwork.

monologue (mon' ə log) *noun* A speech by one character in a play, which reveals the character's thoughts and feelings. Also called a *soliloquy.*

opera (op' ə re) *noun* A work of musical drama in which the characters sing rather than speak. An opera includes singers and musicians, and often includes dancers.

perspective (pûr spek' tiv) *noun* An artist's use of line and space in ways that suggest real-world distances. *Changing the size of figures in a drawing is one way to show perspective. For example, smaller figures seem farther away and larger figures appear closer.*

pigment (pig' mənt) *noun* A substance used for coloring, often a powder mixed with liquid.

primary colors (prī' mer' ē kul' ərz) *plural noun* The three basic colors that can be combined to create all other colors. In pigments for paints, the primary colors are red, yellow, and blue. In inks used for printing, the primary colors are magenta (purplish red), yellow, and cyan (greenish blue).

proportion (prə pôr' shən) *noun* The relation of one element in an artwork to another, in terms of size or number. *Draw the arms of a figure in proportion to the body.*

secondary colors (sek' ən der' ē kul' ərz) *plural noun* Colors made by mixing equal amounts of primary colors. *Mix red and yellow to get the secondary color orange.*

Important Art Words I Need to Know

symphony (sim' fə nē) *noun* A long piece of music with at least three sections called movements. A symphony is composed for a large group of musicians known as a symphony orchestra.

texture (teks' cher) *noun* The appearance and feel of a surface. *Oil paints applied thickly have a rough texture.*

tragedy (traj' i dē) *noun* A play or other dramatic work in which the characters suffer because of their own failings or because of outside forces. Tragedies have unhappy endings.

vanishing point (van' ish ing point) *noun* The place where lines in a scene seem to meet and then disappear. *The road ends at a vanishing point on the horizon.*

Vocabulary Notes

Academic Vocabulary Practice • Grade 5 • CD-104810

Answer Key

Math

Page 6
1. Answers will vary. 2. Answers will vary. 3. Students will research. 4. Answers will vary. 5. 62.8 cm, 12.56 m, 75.36 in.

Page 7
1. expression; 2. expression; 3. equation; 4. expression; 5. equation; 6. equation; 7. expression; 8. equation; 9. expression; 10. expression; 11. equation; 12. expression; *Challenge!* Answers will vary but may include *equal, equate, equator, equilateral.*

Page 8
Answers will vary but may include: *formula*: a number sentence with letters standing for numbers; letters on both sides of an equal sign, such as $A = L \times W$ for finding area; You replace the letters with numbers and find out how long something takes, or how big it is, or other information about amounts. *algebra*: a way to work with equations that include missing numbers shown with letters; an equation that has numbers and letters, such as $2x = 14$; You use algebra to figure out missing numbers.

Page 9
1. 1, 2, 3, 6, composite; 2. 1, 3, 9, composite; 3. 1, 3, 7, 21, composite; 4. 1, 2, 3, 4, 6, 9, 12, 18, 36, composite; 5. 1, 37, prime; 6. 1, 3, 9, 27, 81, composite; 7. 1, 5, 25, composite; 8. 1, 47, prime; 9. 9, 25, 36, 81; *Challenge!* 2, 3, 5, 7, 11, 13, 17, 19, 23, 29, 31, 37, 41, 43, 47, 53, 59, 61, 67, 71, 73, 79, 83, 89, 97, 101, 103, 107, 109, 113, 127, 131, 137, 139, 149, 151, 157, 163, 167, 173, 179, 181, 191, 193, 197, 199

Page 10
Answers will vary but may include: 1. Yes, an integer is any whole number including 0. 2. Yes, (+1,–5) would be in the lower right. 3. No, integers are whole numbers, not parts of numbers. 4. No, the order of the numbers makes a difference in where the point is. 5. Yes, 150 is a whole number.

Page 11
1. A; 2. A; 3. B; 4. A; 5. A; 6. B

Page 12
Answers will vary but may include: 1. No, the average and the median are not the same. 2. Yes, the average and the mean are the same. 3. No, because there might not be a number that appears more often than other numbers. 4. No, because the mean will always be less than the highest number. 5. Yes, there could be a list in which the middle number is the same as the average. 6. Yes, I would want the median score because the middle number would be 95, but the mean score would be lower than that.

Page 13
1. Students' drawings should show a triangle with two equal sides and one angle greater than 90 degrees. 2. Students' drawings should show a triangle with sides of different lengths and no angle 90 degrees or greater. 3. Students' drawings should show a square or other rectangle.

Page 14
Answers spell *geometry.*

Page 15
1. frequency; 2. mode; 3. acute; 4. vertex; 5. formula; 6. isosceles; 7. obtuse; 8. mathematics; 9. sample; 10. integer; Answer to riddle: your mother

Science

Page 17
Answers will vary but may include: *air pressure*: the push of air; a balloon filling up until it bursts; We need air pressure to breathe. *atmosphere*: the gases that surround Earth; blue sky and clouds; The atmosphere protects Earth from the sun's harmful rays and holds the gases needed for life.

Page 18
Answers will vary but may include: 1. he saw that the plants still died even when they had enough sunlight. 2. try to explain what else might cause the weight gain. 3. make a scientific test comparing health when they eat the high-sugar snacks for a period and when they stop eating them for the same period. 4. what is known and what seems likely to be true.
Word Alert! 1. hypotheses; 2. hypothesis

Page 19
1. tendon, tissue; 2. ligament; 3. ligaments; 4. tendon; 5. tendons; 6. Ligaments; *Challenge!* Answers will vary but may include: Achilles' unprotected heel was famous because of the myth, so the tendon in the heel was named after him.

Page 20
1. radiation; 2. convection; 3. conduction; 4. convection; 5. radiation; 6. conduction; 7. Answers will vary but may include an electric iron. 8. Answers will vary but may include a convection oven. 9. Answers will vary but may include a fluorescent lamp. 10. to behave in the same way as others; 11. to meet with others; 12. with the same size and shape, or to match with something else

Answer Key

Page 21
1. opaque; 2. transparent; 3. translucent; 4. opaque;
5. transparent; 6. translucent; Answers will vary
but may include: 7. clean water; 8. a shower door;
9. heavy fabric; *Word Alert!* Answers will vary but may
include: 10. Light rays pass through a translucent
material, but objects appear blurry. 11. Light passes
through a transparent material, and objects are clear.
12. To transmit a signal is to send it across air or space.
13. To transfer something is to move it from one place
to another.

Page 22
1. B; 2. B; 3. A; 4. B; 5. A; *Look It Up!* Students' words
and drawings should show that *photo-* means "light,"
and *synthesis* means "putting together."

Page 23
1. Sepals; 2. petals; 3. stigma; 4. stamen; 5. ovary;
6. filament; 7. anther; 8. style

Page 24
1. metamorphic; 2. sedimentary; 3. igneous;
4. metamorphic; 5. igneous; 6. sedimentary;
7. Answers will vary but may include slate. 8. Answers
will vary but may include shale. 9. Answers will vary but
may include pumice. 10. F; 11. T; 12. T

Page 25
Answers will vary but may include: 1. makes a
molecule of carbon dioxide. 2. one or more negatively
charged particles called electrons spin around the
nucleus. 3. combine chemically to form a compound.
4. any other element, such as oxygen or iron. 5. made
of atoms that are much too tiny to see.

Page 26
Answers will vary but may include: 1. No, we see a
reflection of light. 2. No, we see only the wavelengths
of visible light. 3. Yes, and it is broken into colors. 4. No,
it refracts light but does not break it into colors. 5. Yes,
the light bends as it passes from air into water.

Page 27
Answers will vary but may include: 1. The vertebrae of
the neck protect the spinal cord and connect to the
skull. 2. Sensory neurons in the skin send signals to the
spinal cord and the brain—"pain." 3. Sensory neurons
in the nose send messages about smells to the spinal
cord and the brain. 4. Motor nerves will soon send a
message to the person's muscles—"jump." *Challenge!*
Guide students in finding a research source that
names the groupings: cervical, thoracic, lumbar,
sacral, coccygeal.

Page 28
Answers spell *chemical.*

Page 29
Answers spell *conclusion.*

Technology

Page 31
Students use this page to assess their own knowledge
of *design process.* Encourage students to explain how
their drawings help them remember word meanings.

Page 32
Answers will vary but may include: *Name*:
Telecommunications involve communicating, or
sending messages, over distances. *Examples*: texting,
instant-messaging, email; *Effects*: instant contact,
constant contact; *Changes*: much faster than mailing
letters or sending telegrams, reach many people
at once

Page 33
Answers will vary but may include: 1. A useful interface
must be easy to understand, such as the one on the
right. 2. It is the software that communicates between
the computer and the printer. 3. The words and
the pictures are easy to understand, and the steps to
follow are clearly laid out. 4. clicking on icons on the
desktop, scrolling, dragging, and using shortcut
keyboard commands. *Word Alert!* Answers will vary
but may include: The interface is between a computer
and a person or another machine.

Page 34
Answers will vary but may include: 1. This desk does not
move unless I push it. 2. It is much harder to push the
teacher's desk than to push my desk. 3. A toy car that
has been pushed will stop rolling unless it gets another
push. 4. If I need to stop my bike suddenly, I have to
squeeze the hand brakes really hard. To stop slowly, I
squeeze gently.

Page 35
1. potential energy; 2. potential energy; 3. kinetic
energy; 4. potential energy; 5. kinetic energy; 6. kinetic
energy; 7. potential energy; 8. potential energy;
Challenge! Answers will vary but may include: a
sculpture or mobile that moves.

Page 36
1. template; 2. prototype; 3. templates; 4. template;
5. prototype; Answers will vary but may include: 6. to
make sure the machine will work right and that each
completed one will work the same. 7. engineers can
test a model. 8. make the actual machines.

Answer Key

Page 37
1. spreadsheet; 2. database; 3. spreadsheet; 4. spreadsheet; 5. database; 6. database; Answers will vary but may include: 7. The user can use a search term to find any entry in the spreadsheet, so it is a kind of database. *Word Alert!* 8. Answers will vary but may include: the columns and rows of cells that can be filled in with words and numbers; 9. Answers will vary but may include: You go to one central source to find any kind of information it holds.

Page 38
1. B; 2. B; 3. A; 4. B; 5. A; 6. B; *Look It Up!* Answers will vary but may include: 7. a group of TV stations that show the same programs at the same time; 8. two or more computers that are linked with cables or wirelessly

Page 39
Answers will vary but may include: 1. Yes, when you talk or send pictures or text, it sends those signals to receivers on cell towers. 2. No, a satellite circles Earth. 3. No, a TV receives signals but does not send them. 4. No, a receiver does not send signals. 5. No, a satellite receiver is shown. The satellite is in space. 6. Yes, many cars have satellite radio systems. *Look It Up!* Answers will vary but may include: natural satellites and artificial ones

Page 40
Answers will vary but may include: 1. rushing water does not run out as long as rain continues to fill rivers. 2. it is spinning and has energy of motion. 3. electrical energy. 4. driving the generator. 5. magnets and wires. 6. the water has a lot of mechanical energy. *Challenge!* Answers will vary but may include: The shared word parts are *hydro* (water) and *therm* (heat).

Page 41
Answers spell *teamwork*.

Page 42
1. two computers; 2. math operations; 3. library catalog; 4. electronic signals; 5. design process; 6. rotating machine; 7. word processing; 8. numerical data; Riddle and answer: What is as light as a feather, yet you can't hold it for two minutes? (your breath)

Language Arts

Page 44
Answers will vary but may include: *autobiography*: a person's own story of his or her life; What was my childhood like? How did I accomplish what I did? What challenges did I face? I grew up in a poor village, dreaming of getting an education. *bibliography*: a list of sources used for a nonfiction work; Where were the facts for this book found? Who was interviewed? How up-to-date are the sources? Arnold, Caroline. <u>Giant Sea Reptiles of the Dinosaur Age</u>. NY: Clarion, 2007. *Word Alert!* Answers will vary but may include: 1. "Biblio" has to do with books, so a bibliography is a list of books. "Bio" has to do with life, so a biography is the story of a life. 2. A biography is the story of a life, but the prefix "auto-" adds the meaning "self," so an autobiography is the story of one's own life.

Page 45
Answers will vary but may include: 1. Your clothes will be the whitest they have ever been if you use Cleano! 2. We shouted even more loudly, but no one heard us. 3. Home-baked cookies are tastier than store-bought ones. 4. The Eagles were better last year than the year before, but they are having their best season right now. 5. Change *worsest* to *worst*—there is no such word as *worsest*.

Page 46
1. colon; insert colon after each greeting. 2. colon; insert colon after *items* and after *idea*. 3. semicolon; insert semicolon after *tonight*. 4. semicolon; Replace comma with semicolon after *France* and *England*. 5. semicolon; colon; *Challenge!* Answers will vary.

Page 47
Answers will vary but may include: 1. for, under; 2. Wow; Amazing! 3. My, yours; 4. by, on, with; 5. *Oh,* interjection; *in,* preposition; *its,* possessive pronoun

Page 48
1. Answers will vary but may include: I swam across the pool. 2. <u>were barking</u>; 3. Answers will vary but may include: My friend is walking fast. 4. <u>had left</u>; circle *had*; leave; 5. Change *went* to *gone* because the verb *go* is irregular. The form used with a helping verb is *gone*. *Look It Up!* Answers will vary but may include: tense—worried and nervous; tense—form of verb that expresses past, present, or future

Page 49
1. B; 2. A; 3. B; 4. A; 5. A; 6. A; *Word Alert!* 1. generalization; 2. general; 3. generalize; 4. generally

Page 50
1. first person; 2. second person; 3. third person; 4. first person; 5. Answers will vary.

Answer Key

Page 51
Answers will vary but may include: **1.** between icicles and long fingers is a personification that makes the icicles seem like a person. **2.** one way to build suspense is by using foreshadowing to hint at what might happen. **3.** personification are kinds of figurative language that authors use. **4.** an author will take the reader back in time to show what happened earlier. **5.** a narrative does not have to be fiction. It can also be a true story.

Page 52
Answers will vary but may include: **1.** Yes, although you can read a drama too. **2.** No, a tall tale is a kind of funny folktale and does not have the supernatural beings of a myth. **3.** No, a science fiction story could take place in the past or the present. **4.** Yes, historical fiction is about something that happened in the past. **5.** No, a poem is a kind of writing in the genre of poetry. **6.** Yes, a myth often has heroes who face monsters or other dangers. **7.** Yes, if the historical fiction takes place when he was alive. **8.** No, an author could write *in* a genre.

Page 53
1. persuasive essay; **2.** introduction; **3.** transitions; **4.** conclusion; **5.** revisions; *Word Alert!* Answers will vary but may include: *introduce, transit, conclude, revise*

Page 54
1-4. Answers will vary but must connect with the stories.

Page 55
Answers spell *literary.*

Page 56
Answers spell is *knowledgeable.*

Social Studies

Page 58
Answers will vary but may include: **1.** cooperation, partnership, agreement, teamwork; **2.** European Union; United Nations; NATO; trading partners such as Canada and the United States; Britain, France, and the United States in world wars; **3.** to become stronger by working together for a shared goal or against a threat; **4.** sign a treaty; have meetings with diplomats; build on past friendships; make marriages between ruling families

Page 59
Answers will vary but may include: *Name:* US citizens vote for the people who will represent them and govern them. *Describing words:* democratic, self-governing, representative; *Reasons:* gives people a

say in their government; limits power of rulers; *Differences:* Not all nations are republics. A nation might have a different form of government such as a dictatorship or a monarchy.

Page 60
Answers will vary.

Page 61
1. aggression; **2.** negotiation; **3.** aggression; **4.** negotiation; **5.** negotiation; *Word Alert!*
1. negotiator; **2.** negotiate; **3.** negotiable; **4.** negotiation

Page 62
Answers will vary but may include: **1.** the workers come to live near the factories, and more buildings and stores are built. **2.** families crowded into apartment buildings and streets filled with people and vehicles. **3.** the pollution caused by burning fuel to power factories. **4.** people purchased manufactured goods in big department stores. *Word Alert!* **5.** industry + -al + -ize + -ation = industrialization; **6.** urban + -ize + -ation = urbanization

Page 63
1. B; **2.** A; **3.** A; **4.** B; **5.** B; **6.** B

Page 64
Answers will vary but may include: **1.** No, it is controlled by a foreign government. **2.** No, colonization takes place on foreign soil. **3.** Yes, missionaries represented their churches. **4.** No, an expedition can be on land. **5.** No, forming a colony means building a settlement, but a settlement is not always a colony.
Challenge! Answers will vary but may include: During colonial times, European rulers wanted colonization of distant lands, so they sent colonists to set up a colony.

Page 65
Answers will vary but may include: **1.** No, they just did not want a central government that was too powerful. **2.** Yes, in a compromise, each side gives up something. **3.** No, seceding is the opposite of joining. **4.** Yes, they all wanted to abolish slavery. **5.** Yes, both names are used for the war. *Look It Up!* Answers will vary but may include: A civil war is any fighting between the people of the same country; the particular war that took place in the United States is known as the Civil War.

Answer Key

Page 66
Answers will vary but may include: **1.** that group to feel mistreated and possibly fight back. **2.** get an education and job skills and have a say in their own government. **3.** the company will lose so much money that it will change its ways of doing business. **4.** a struggle, because they were working hard but earning little money and still under the control of landowners. **5.** people never forget the suffering they and their family members went through. They might stay angry and want revenge. **6.** that the much larger southern farms were worked by slave laborers.

Page 67
1. A; **2.** B; **3.** B; **4.** B; **5.** B

Page 68
Answers spell *heritage*.

Page 69
Answers spell *historians*.

Geography

Page 71
Answers will vary but may include: **1.** The Pacific Plate and the North American Plate are tectonic plates that meet to create the San Andreas Fault, where earthquakes occur. **2.** The large land masses called continents rest on moving pieces of Earth's outer layer. **3.** It is one of the big, somewhat thin sections of crust and upper mantle. *Challenge!* Answers will vary but may include: Tectonic plates are the moving parts of Earth's outer layer. Plate tectonics is the scientific theory that explains the movement of continents.

Page 72
Answers will vary but may include: *Local terrain*: low hills, rocky hillsides, river valley; *Describing words*: level, steep, rocky, dry, soggy, coastal; *Why they matter*: make a difference for preparing the ground for farming, for building roads and homes, for traveling safely; *Terrain/territory*: Both have the root *terr-*, which has to do with land.

Page 73
1. latitude; **2.** longitude; **3.** longitude; **4.** longitude; **5.** latitude; **6.** longitude; **7.** longitude; **8.** longitude

Page 74
1. B; **2.** A; **3.** A; **4.** A; **5.** A

Page 75
Answers will vary but may include: **1.** they circle the globe without ever meeting. **2.** move long distances during the dry season in search of grass. **3.** can vary from very moist to very dry. **4.** far to the north or south of the tropical zone. **5.** some desert regions get almost no rainfall all year. **6.** it is not as dry as a desert and not as wet as a rain forest.

Page 76
Answers will vary but may include: **1.** has an extremely high population density. **2.** cannot be drawn at true scale, although map projections can show relative sizes and distances. **3.** the annexation of land such as Alaska. **4.** the political boundary between the countries of Libya and Algeria.

Page 77
Answers spell *rainfall*.

Page 78
Answers spell *geographer*.

Civics and Economics

Page 80
Students use this page to assess their own knowledge of *entrepreneur*. Encourage students to explain how their drawings help them remember word meanings.

Page 81
Answers will vary but may include: **1.** different producers focusing on particular products or services; **2.** teacher, doctor, clothing store, clothing manufacturer; **3.** No one person or business could provide all of the things that people need. **4.** They think about what they are interested in doing and choose a training program or school to prepare them. *Word Alert!* Answers will vary but may include: *realization, dramatization*.

Page 82
1. distribution; **2.** distribution; **3.** consumption; **4.** distribution; **5.** consumption; **6.** consumption; **7.** consumption; **8.** distribution

Page 83
1. low, high, high; **2.** high, low, low; **3.** low, high, high; **4.** high, low, low; **5.** high, low, low; **6.** low, high, high; **7.** low, high, high; **8.** high, low, low; **9.** low, high, high; **10.** high, low, low

Page 84
Answers will vary but may include: **1.** are allowed to gather; **2.** document requesting action; **3.** urge; **4.** get permission from; **5.** cannot meet; **6.** amendment; Answers will vary but may include: **7.** a crowd turns into a violent mob. **8.** wanted the principal to change a school rule that they thought was unfair.

Answer Key

Page 85
Answers will vary but may include: *majority rule*: used for voting, decision based on just more than half of the votes, fair because it shows view of more voters, unfair because many voters may disagree; *both*: fair treatment for all, rules for people to follow, fair laws, democratic principles; *due process*: law protects people accused of crimes, prevents unfair punishment, accused person has rights—must be informed of what the crime is, have speedy trial, lawyer, jury trial.

Page 86
1. A; 2. A; 3. A; 4. B; 5. A; 6. B
Look It Up! Answers will vary.

Page 87
Answers will vary but may include: 1. No, the Senate is part of Congress. 2. Yes, the House has 435 members, and the Senate has 100 members. 3. Yes, they represent all of the people in their states. 4. Yes, a state with a low population has only one representative but two senators. 5. No, a senator votes in the Senate.
Word Alert! <u>congress</u>ional <u>represent</u>ation; Answers will vary but may include: Members of Congress represent the people in their districts in the system of congressional representation.

Page 88
Answers will vary but may include: 1. can limit the actions of; 2. make sure; 3. passed a law; 4. make decisions; 5. the members; *Word Alert!* Answers will vary but may include: having to do with the laws of the nation

Page 89
Answers spell *assembly*.

Page 90
1. illegal, unlawful; 2. job, profession; 3. trial, case; 4. legislature, congress; 5. delivery; transport; 6. consumption, spending; 7. demand, interest; 8. entrepreneur, boss; 9. petition, address; 10. gathering, rally; *Riddle and answer:* What should you always keep after you give it to someone else? (your word)

Art

Page 92
Students use this page to assess their own knowledge of *harmony*. Encourage students to explain how their drawings help them remember word meanings.

Page 93
Answers will vary but may include: 1. makes up dance steps to music; 2. They study work of other choreographers. They are trained dancers themselves. 3. the beat of the music, the mood of the music, how dancers look as they move together, how each dancer moves every part of his or her body; 4. in musical theaters, with music video makers, on TV dance shows, with ballet companies, anywhere that dancers perform; *Look It Up!* 5. "choral dance" 6. "write" or "writing"

Page 94
1. tragedy; 2. tragedy; 3. comedy; 4. comedy; 5. tragedy; 6. Answers will vary.

Page 95
1. Symphonies, Operas; 2. operas, symphonies; 3. symphonies, operas; 4. operas, Symphonies; 5. Operas, Symphonies; 6. symphonies, opera

Page 96
1. dialogue; 2. monologues; 3. monologue; 4. dialogue; 5. dialogue; 6. monologue; *Word Alert!* Answers will vary but may include: A monotone makes a voice sound boring, so an actor giving a monologue should not bore the audience.

Page 97
Answers will vary but may include: 1. The statue in Monroe Park depicts a Civil War soldier. 2. Picturing a scene means that you form a picture in your mind. Depicting a scene means that you paint it or draw it. 3. It might show zigzag shapes or bursts of color that suggest movement. 4. Drawings will vary. *Challenge!* Guide students in finding art sources.

Page 98
Answers will vary but may include: 1. high heat; 2. plates; 3. surface; 4. kiln; 5. decorative; 6. tradition; 7. clay; 8. chemists

Page 99
1. A; 2. B; 3. B; 4. A; 5. B; 6. A

Page 100
Answers will vary but may include: The artist's use of perspective makes the scene seem 3-D. The artist gives the illusion that the tree is in the front of the scene. The road ends at a vanishing point.

Page 101
Answers will vary but may include: Markers contain pigments. This color wheel shows the primary colors red, yellow, and blue. It shows the secondary colors orange, violet, and green. Yellow and blue are complementary colors. *Challenge!* Guide students in locating information about color wheels, where they may find the term *tertiary colors*.

Page 102
Answers spell *artistry*.

Page 103
Answer is *THEY ENRICH LIFE!*